TECONOMICS OF *DYNAMIC SUSTAINABLE* BUDGETS

Dynamic Sustainable Modular Production Budgets

X

Bahman Fakhraie, Ph.D.

TECONOMICS OF DYNAMIC SUSTAINABLE BUDGETS

Teconomics of Dynamic Sustainable Budgets

Teconomic of Dynamic Sustainable Strategic Budgeting: From Small to Large Operational Modular Production-Models

By

Bahman Fakhraie, PhD

7/15//2013

ISBN: 978-0-9894539-1-2
Library of Congress copyright
Case Number, 11023570364

$89.98
ISBN 978-0-9894539-1-2
58998>
9 780989 453912

Acknowledgments

Many thanks, to family and friends. Bahman married Kay Davis 1976, master in Speech Pathology from Utah State University. His daughter, Lara Fatemeh Fakhraie, earned her Master's degree from Oregon State University. She is a published author. She resides in Oregon. His son, Anayat Fakhraie, a screenwriter earned his Master from the American Film Institute, and he is a member of WGAW. They did their undergraduate work at University of Utah. Fakhraie families have endured revolutions, death of family, and hardships. The sui generis caravan of joy de vive continues. I wish for all of the family members, professors, teachers, students, helpers, and friends spread all over the globe my best wishes, warm thoughts, and many thanks. Life events are neither fair nor even. I wish you will learn from them, and they would always leave you better off than before.

Abstract

All production processes have some inherent risks. Financial risks increase substantially, to restate an old idiomatic phrase, if you fail to budget, as part of your economic plan for the modular production operations, you will plan to fail your budgets. An important part of innovation development of new process of technological innovations was learning to master the exceptions to the rules, which reduce risks.

Therefore, an important part of gestalt of new technological injections, and new variables of modular production processes precede almost all thought action processes, and it is the budgeting of the modular-operations. Dr. Bahman Fakhraie studied the endogenous elements of modular production process. He introduced the new variable as the educational aspect of human capital skills, which among other things would also reduce some risks. The scientific difference among the mammals and other species are the capabilities to learn group planning and defense, or individual survival tricks and skills, then retain that knowledge, and pass on those skills to improve the chance for their offspring survivals, in the more general genome survival and continuations.

The dynamic sustainable budgeting skills are among those top skills in operation of modular production models, which have evolved since development of cave-barters and village bazars, and the Persians mud-sphere record keeping along evolutionary knowledge development of human history.

Contents

List of Tables

List of Figures

Preface

Dr. Bahman Fakhraie, PhD in economics, University of Utah, his dissertation added to the influences of the Unorthodox Holistic Economic doctrine and complemented the modern Orthodox economic theories, in the millennial age of technological paradigm shifts. He applies analytical skills with gestalt study of history, mathematics, and econometrics to economic analysis, with scientific background in his books. He is a published economist, author, researcher, investor, and private contractor. His skills are in international trade and finance, economic production (theory and application), growth and development theory, econometrics, agriculture economics, and agronomy.

The readers will note the organization of this book fallows the development denoted in figure 3, dynamic budget spreadsheet, with new ideas and theoretical advancement added to chapters. This book is the result of many years of notes and journals, studies, learned skills, and exceptions to the rules, which Dr. Bahman Fakhraie wrote and accumulated at works and businesses, and complemented, by years of education since (1960s).

Dr. Bahman Fakhraie developed the formulaic presentations of dynamic budgeting in these forms very recently. They are presentable in older skill with pen and papers (since 1975) to more recent formats. They can use these formulations. The softwares are (Sunbeam Microsystem Inc., OpenOffice.org software, or the professional Microsoft office, Excel) language of spreadsheet EXCEL (X), which is now, included with windows and apple operating systems.

Dr. Bahman Fakhraie was invited by Senator Frank M. Browning to attend Utah State University, when Senator visited his family. After his master, he attended the

University of Utah for the Ph.D. program in economics. He has met most of modern day science, business, and economic opinion leaders, and few other stars of their own fields. Dr. Bahman Fakhraie's book web page is at following link: http://bahfecon.wix.com/bahfecon.

CHPTER 1

Teconmics of Dynamic Budgeting

The process of living is a continuum. Life and activity of living organisms are dynamic, too. Organisms as active and complex as honeybees and farm ants, and as singularly active as humming birds, they all budget their intake of calories, energy, and food cultivations to maintain their activities, their lives, and feed their progenies. They choose and modify their activities with respect to location, collection of food, and life events in survival, confrontation, and, genetic continuum (procreations), with a dynamic teconomic budgeting in their natural routines. The new frontiers of sciences we have discovered are new studies of the old endowed nature.

Historically, with mathematics and algebra in Persia, very limited parts of these formulations were calculated.[1] That was also a giant leap of record keeping technology, and knowledge advancement at its time.

The root of the word budget also goes to 15th century middle Europe, Middle English bowgette, middle French bougette or boulge for belly and leather bag.[2] Student of archeology know that goat belly floats sown and filled with air, then used to float between Persia and Mesopotamia on daily trade.[3] The modern simple definition refers to a stock amount of money required to do certain projects for a given amount of time.[4] There are complex definition, about statement of financial position, and economic resources like energy that is for certain purpose or demand for a certain period. In temporal economic analysis, the complex issues as injections of time, stock and flow factors, are presented.

However, modern methodologies have evolved to allow complex adaptation of spreadsheets, finance, personal economics, and budgeting as new scientific tools.

That means it will meet the following scientific requirements,

1. It allows for hypothetical (true/false) testing,
2. It allows for repeated recalculations,
3. It allows multigenerational data analysis,
4. It allows multi-technology analysis,
5. It allows multi-methodology analysis,
6. It allows for (Popperian) verifiability,
7. It allows for falsification and rejection.

Therefore, it meets modern criteria for scientific definitions, including Popperian criteria.

Human endeavors are dynamic series of modular productions individuals arranged, first for survival, then competition for food, self-defense, and warfare. Later, the trades by caravans and by sea developed complex economic and business activities, which required record keepings. These necessities evolved the more demands in modern age of economic growth and developmental plans and progress. Thus, it has advanced the new digital or computer age of record keeping, and budgeting.

All modular productions in series of productions require atomized budgeting and dynamic assessments of their viabilities, risk associated with them. The farmer ants and honeybees we mentioned have modular production, in food search, storage, in defense of hive, the queen, and embryonic members, the numbers and natures of modular productions changes in rest time, or at food finding as well. In human commercial activities in economics, we use to study this under a general topic of production theory, in optimum utilizations of resources by workers, and capital to produce the output for services and consumptions good.

The important modern discoveries in this book and in the last few books are the development of modular productions, which entail main industry production. The fiscal theory and international trade applications of modular productions were advanced in filmic and auto industries.[5]

This book develops the significance of dynamic budgets, in 'Teconomics of Dynamic Sustainable Budgets' in series of modular productions in each industry. Thus, it guarantees possibilities of the essential parts, before we get to sustainable functionality of the holistic combinations.

Since there are risks and uncertainties associated with the modular production processes, Teconomic of dynamic budgeting are essential components of advancement of human capital skills. In the same category of important technological injections of human capitals, as education and research of financial risks, which enhance returns, profits, and rewards of modular productive investments, and reduce chances and occurrences of risk associated with such endeavors.

Teconomic of dynamic budgeting presents foundational tools to evaluate and construct teconomics and analytical constructs.[6] A well-constructed dynamic budget sorts the viabilities of the processes, which combined human and non-human capital and resources in numbers of modular production processes for optimum production of needed or wanted products with maximum profitability for a given period.

Introduction

The gestalt of new technologies injections and new variables of all modular production processes can continue, after almost all of the essential initial thought-action sequences of productions.[7] Dr. Bahman Fakhraie introduced in his studies the endogenous elements of production process and the new variables that were the educational aspect of skills, which among other things they would reduce some risks.[8] Otherwise, humanity first thought action modular production process would have halted.

That is, the first hominids would have not stepped out of the caves because of risks in becoming fast food for dinosaurs, large cats, and predators. Therefore, partial comprehension of food supply, energy, and external conditions were used to evaluate the time, speed, and location, and quantity of hunting and gathering required.

Even at those elemental levels, at hunting and gathering level of competence in human endeavors these were needed for the hard lives of early ancestors. All supplies and access to energy sources were limited. Uses of honey, fruit, and food-fats were available after accumulated skills were acquired.

That is teconomic of dynamic budgeting at work to reduce risk and increase sustainability and continuity of productive operations for different aspect of the hunting and gathering in process, or more complex modern modular production units.[9]

Since, these fields are fresh and dynamically changing, and unpredictable, this study is by no mean exhaustive, nor any study can be at this stage of knowledge accumulations. Therefore, this is a testimonial to the needs for the study, and that fact that no guarantees are given legal or academic.

Budgeting

The elemental steps in determining what resources are available to be used in the most beneficial productive activities.

In constructing a new budget spreadsheet, labels, organization of the blank spreadsheet, and segmentations require some initial thought, which meets the economic definition. The optimum uses of minimum amount of resources used to achieve maximum amount of output is the definition of economics, which budgeting will assist to organize at each medullar production levels, toward the holistic concept of production.

The evolution of promissory verbal agreements, to ancient notes, to banking T-accounts describes liabilities and assets.[10] In addition, record keeping for asset and liability ledgers of T-accounts served as an early template for our modern technological leap to spreadsheet dynamic budgeting in this book.[11] Therefore, the importance of record keeping is re-emphasized.

Budgeting in Spreadsheets

The initial, upper segment gives its title, date, and copyright information. Figure 1 shows the view of spreadsheet and the selected initial cell C2.

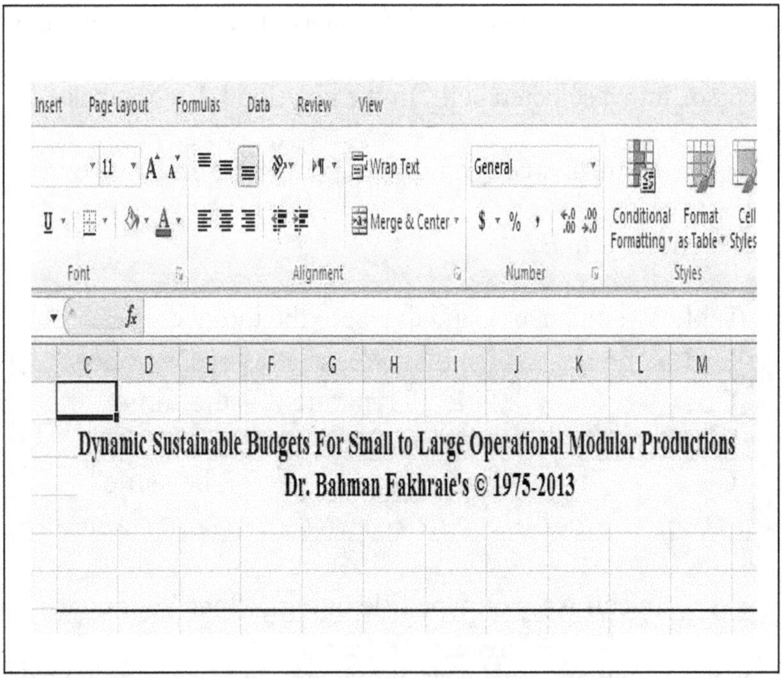

Figure 1, Writing the title in the selected cell C2.

The first step is to open a blank excel spreadsheet file. Then click on save as, and enter the name of your budgeting file. Then, save the spreadsheet, immediately. Now you can reopen the same file Budget 101, and start constructing your budget. Initially, students have to be patient with these early steps, and advance with trial and errors.

After, reopening file Budget101, you will move the cursor into a selected cell. In the position B1, copy/past, or type you title and copyright with your name and date one line under it, in B2.

Table 1, Title, name, and date, are the initial entries.

Cell name	Type or Select	Appearance
C2	Title, "Dynamic.."	the same
C3	Name © date	The same

In cell A4, you type title or tag. Move your curser over one cell and type year, move your curser one more cell and write the year, in our example 2020.

The next few cells for 2021 to 2028, you have two choices. Choice 1 is to write the years one by one in each cell until you the last cell 2028. Choice 2 is the formulaic approach. The latter approach is used for an introductory start in use of formula.

In cell C4, type 2020. Move over one cell, in cell D4, type [= Cd+1] without the brackets. The written matters inside the brackets are the formula. Click in cell D4, then right click>copy. Left click in E4 to K4. Then, left click the option menu appears, click paste, years 2021 to 2028 will appear.

Congratulation you just used formulaic approach to set dates. It can get more complicated, but as long as, you understand the steps by step approach in spreadsheet formulations, and use of text and formula both, you can manage the complications.

Now it is time to put a dividing line under the same line (check figure 3). So, left click on A4, keep your finger on the left click and move the cursor from A4 all the way to K4. A rectangular cell formation remains. Left click in that rectangular. The option menu pops up. Choose bottom border, a small window with a darker black line under it. Left click on that bottom border and a line appears across A4 to K4.

Figure 2 shows The Title, author's name and copyright notice of the budget, starting in cell C2.

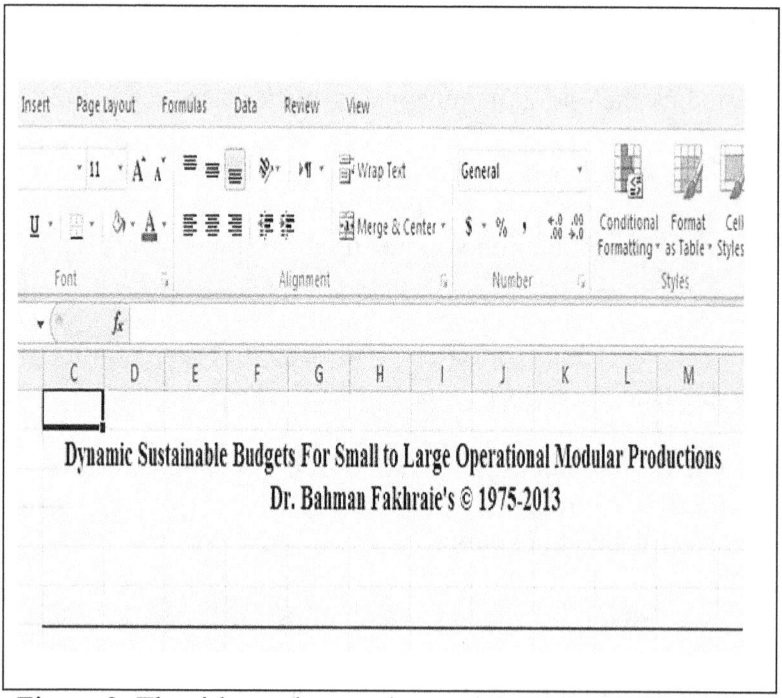

Figure 2, The title, author, and copyright notice of budget.

In the next sections, the overview and structure of the spreadsheet budgeting are presented.

Overview of Budget Spreadsheets

Figure 3 shows the overall view of dynamic sustainable budget. The lessons in presentation of formulas will follow the chapters as identified in this graph.

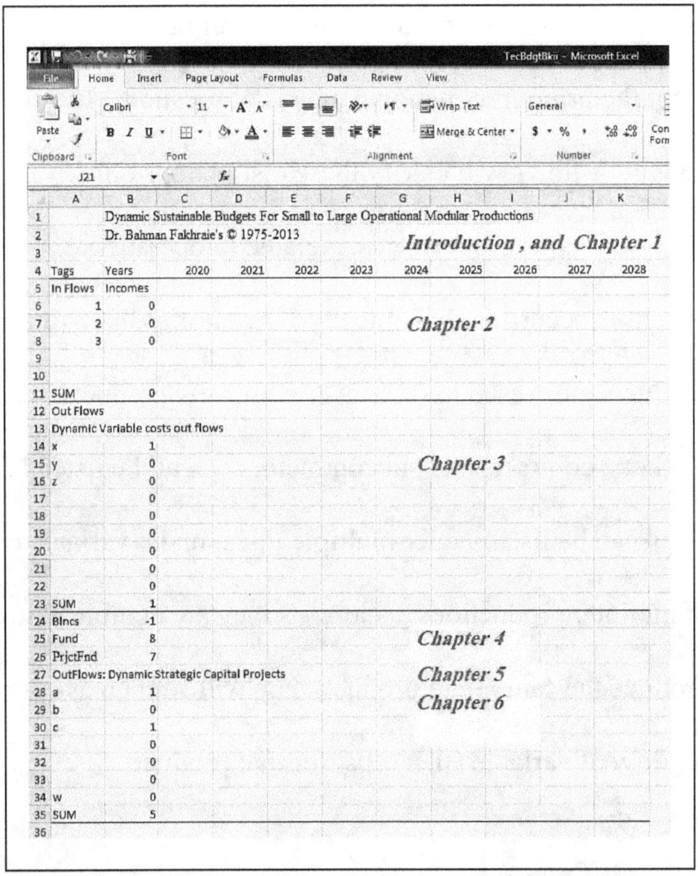

Figure 3, Overall view of the budget spreadsheet.

Therefore, introduction and chapters give an overview of teconomic of dynamic life cycle budgeting, and cover the upper most portion of the budget in this book. The instructions are directed mostly to those matters.

Chapter 2 deals with the income or incomes revenues that make the operations possible. A one-salary family differs from multi-products small business, or manufacturing multinational mega cooperation. The budget in-flows will clarify these distinctions quickly.

Chapter 3 shows costs related to operational expenses occurring dynamically. Inventories, half-finished products purchased to be converted in new products, the workers, contracts and subcontractors can all be listed here. They can be listed under multiple titles, under variable cost of modular productions, as long as they are combined to produce the same final product, they will sum up as outflow of variable (flex) cost for that product.

The reason they are flex or variable costs, is because they can be modify increased or decreased as demand and inflow fluctuates. However, decreases are associated with purchase of fewer inputs, which will affect the final production. An example, when a small farmer employs less planting day workers, plants less acreages of certain annual cash crop.

Chapters 4, 5, 6, are the more advanced part of this book. In the simplest form, the family kinds of budgets chapter 4 will add the inflows and outflows, and keep the end-sum positive as saving weekly, bi-weekly, monthly and annually.

Nevertheless, real lives are more complicated than that. There are education-loans, car-Loans, home mortgages, investment loans, and money you borrowed from mom and dad.

In cases of dynamic modular operational productions, we will add capital maintenance improvements. That means fixing old parts. The other purchases are the capital improvements as up-grades to the budget. That means buying new and improved parts to replace older parts. Since they need savings or saved funds from the current inflows for temporal planed purchases, there will be carry-overs and added interests' incomes each year, or each period.

In chapter 7, some useful legal instruments are detailed. The summery and conclusion are also presented.

Directional impacts of budget numbers

In a household's budget, and small operational budgets, it is easier to see that budget numbers are the result of studied and experiences of the individual involved, but they are alerted, replaced, adjusted, by actual numbers. As, these better numbers become available. In most cases, budgets are modified at three junctures, theoretically.

The income or inflows can change in either direction. Individuals can get a new part time job, and find a job that will affect his or her inflow dramatically. The famed Friday night pink sheet can reduce his or her income substantially, too.

Small businesses have to sell products. Thus, their inflow will be from sales of their products. A large number of government contractors operations get their inflow from form contracts with the government entities. All governments at local, state, national, or global get their inflow from taxes, or regardless of the importance and essentialities of their services, the incomes are disguised fees and taxes. Those taxes and fees are paid from the overall national incomes or inflows, and employed people nationally.

The most likely scenario, which most family deal with is in the flex spending discussions. Some of these choices are types of meat, hamburgers or steak, rice or spaghettis, eating in or movie and dinners. Other harder choices about personal budgets are among, rent, cell phone bill, utilities, electric, and gas bills. Therefore, the most common advice to household budget warriors is pay yourselves (saving, IRAs) and these utilities essential fixed costs first.

What you save here will affect your future consumptions, therefore adds to your forward dynamic planning, it will also improve the chance to make adjustment in current and future capital maintenance and capital upgrades. An important capital is human capital and it is your educational advancement and employable skills. Therefore, your temporal consumption and investment decisions will become a multidirectional advancement in your operational capabilities, and your personal lives.

Dynamic strategic capital maintenances and capital upgrades are the vacuous part of many low-income households' budgets, while it is the most probable method of advancing their lives.

Poverty is often used as an excuse to demonstrate why developmental advancement cannot take shape. It is also misused as a pernicious weapon of upper class warfare against the weaker elements of societies to fight against balanced tax revenue generations to deal with social problems, social goods, infrastructural improvements, and services. Two modern economies have use these methods of wealth concentrations, over the legitimate methods of wealth creation, with jobs, and livable salaries, which encourages higher velocity of money, and balanced exchanges to distributive sustainability along with economic progression at a natural rate, which can self-implode the economy.

Nevertheless, many poor, one-gender families have shown income flow increases with microloans and some initial education (technological-injections).

Figure 4 shows the simple model, and the directional impacts of the budget numbers.

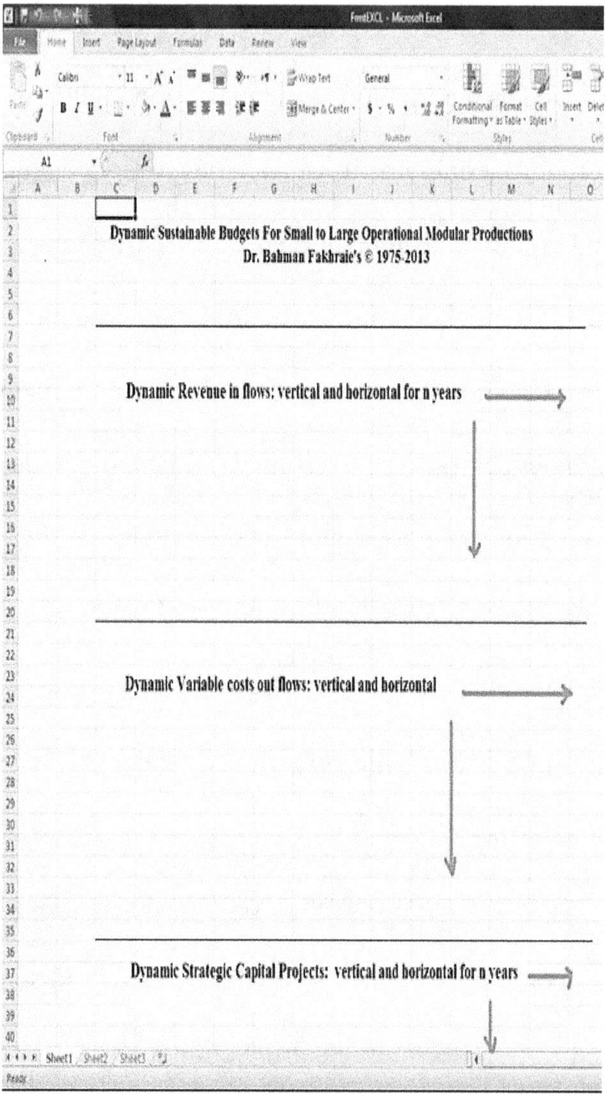

Figure 4, Model of directional impacts of the budget numbers.

Examples are many in USA advanced economy and Bangladesh, one of the poorest countries of the globe. Since the initial studies and introductory research, author did in microloans and developmental agricultural economic theories at Utah State University; in Logan Utah USA 1970-80 (including an unpublished master thesis), the practice has gained recognition and notoriety, because of the accumulated successes, commercial profitability, and lower defaults rates.

Some capital maintenances are not too pricy and can be practices in most modern budget. For example, replacing burned light bulbs, with more efficient lights are common. However, the more expensive alterations are presented in the capital upgrade part of budget, which are more difficult for most limited family budgets.

There are capital purchases that will have temporal impact on future spending in household budgets,

- Purchase of new air conditioners with efficiency units that save on future electrical bills.
- Purchase of new efficiency heating units, washers, dryers, and dishwashers that reduces the utility bills.
- Purchase of new and more efficient cars, which use less or no petroleum in daily commute to jobs.
- Use of new technologies that allows less use of water and irrigation, while it maintains the yard or orchards green alive and productive.

It is important to get understand the necessity and contributions of this scholarly study in dynamic budgeting in complex modern lives of individuals, households, and small modular production associated with small businesses and firms.

Life Cycles of Cash Flow

Individuals as economic agents perform different economic task during their lives, depending where they are in their life cycles. There is a long history of economic theories covering the lifecycle implication of dissaving, saving and investment and dissaving or transfer of real assets as age advances. In temporal economic analysis, we have to study the complex issues injections of time, stock and flow factors, and real and nominal numbers add to the decision matrix for solutions. Some of these decisions are,

1. Education and retraining
2. Job, small business, taxes
3. Saving and investment and retirement
4. Retirement and emergency funds
5. Legacy and inheritance trust funds

Figure 5 teconomic of dynamic budgeting diagram for individuals and households. They formulate 70 to 80 percent of consumption. It is self-destructive to dismiss or diminish their potentiality in free market economies.

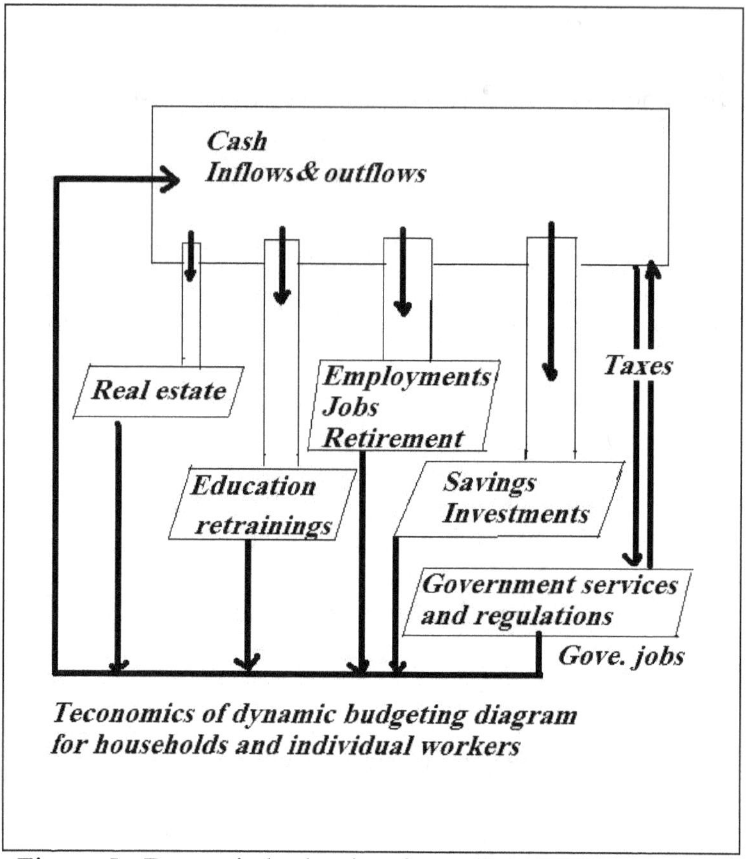

Figure 5, Dynamic budgeting for individuals, households.

Figure 6 shows teconomic of dynamic budgeting diagram for households, and small business engaging in modular production.[12] Figure 7 shows the more complex national model diagram of macroeconomics with most elements.

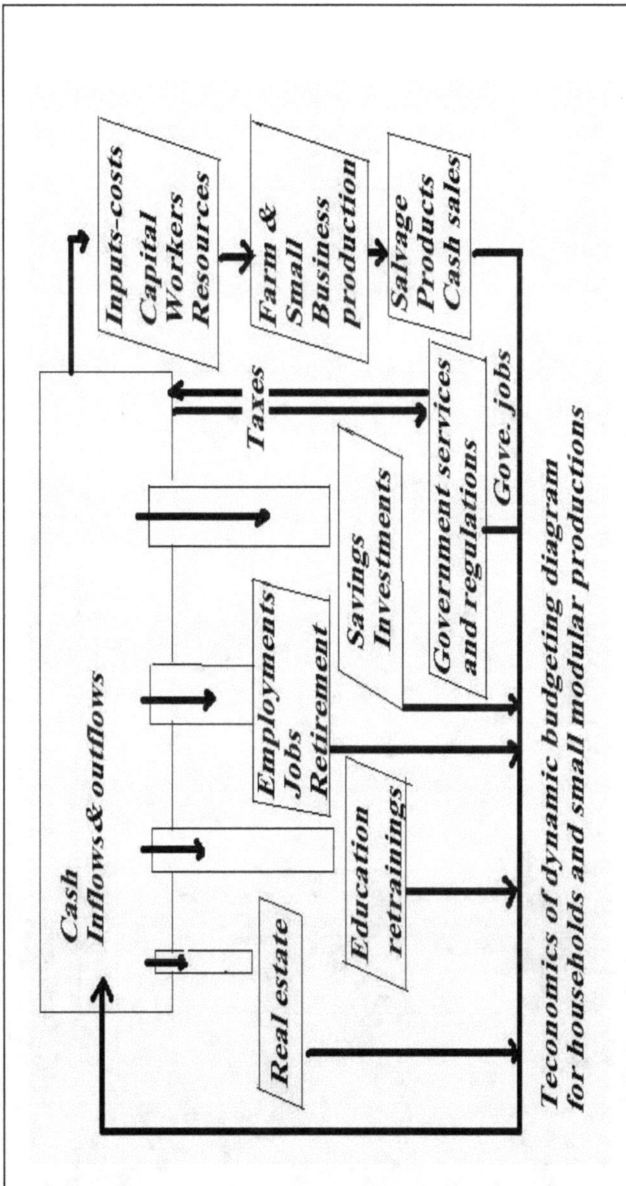

Figure 6, Teconmics of Dynamic budgeting for firms.

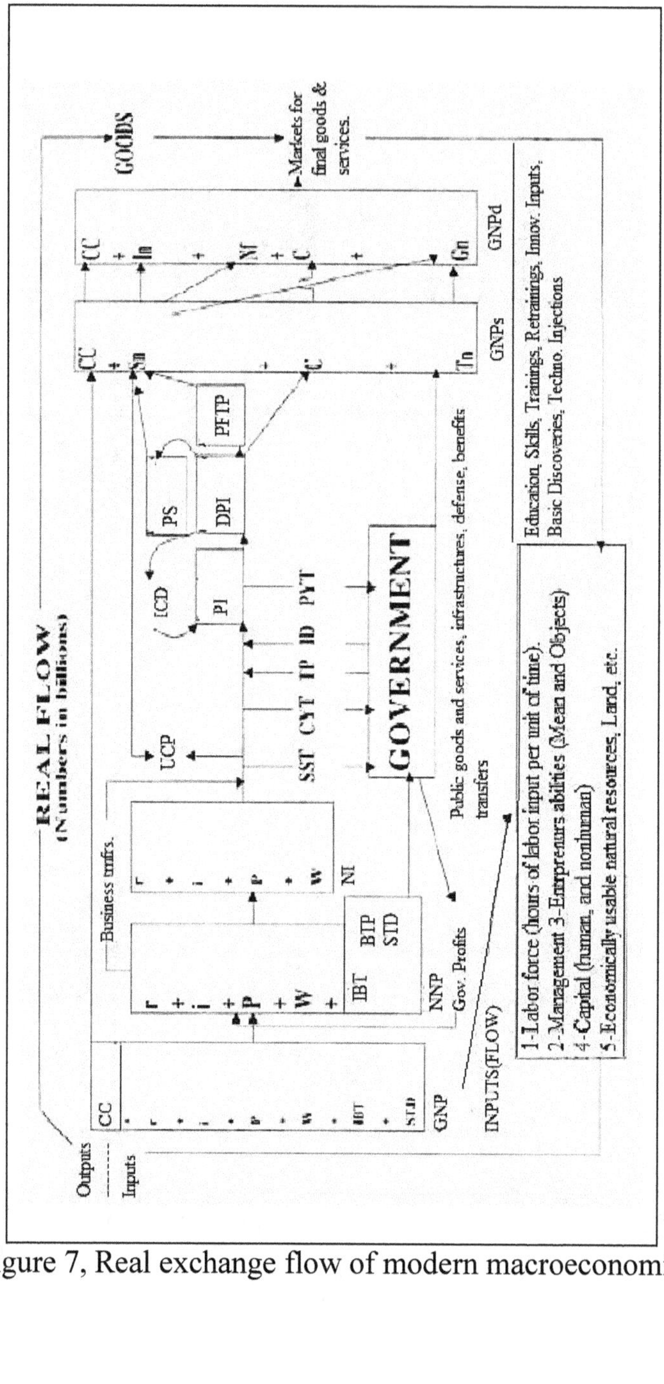

Figure 7, Real exchange flow of modern macroeconomics.

It could be a case of households engaging in small business operation, or the manager of operation dealing with their household budgets. It is also helpful to see that the real national flow diagram exists.

Cash Flow and Life Cycles

How does budgeting, which is so involved in all aspect of modern lives relate to individual economic agents in different stages of their life cycles, from youth to middle age, and old age.

In cases one and two, show how the dissaving in childhood and youth out of the family budgets goes to education and training. That is followed by more saving in middle age years, when employment prospects are good, normally.

Students of teconomic science should observe that it is not a good alternative to underpay workers at this and last stages of life cycles, because burdens of society will increase substantially, as negative externalities accumulate.

Alternatively, adequate or higher real wages will add to intergenerational savings in terms of inherited saving will also add to the next generation potential for increased dissaving. Since in most early adult, that is usually applied to skill expansion, learning, educational training, and improvement of human capital, the positive externalities of that process will increase substantially. This has been missed on a large number of political economics students on the right side of USA political discourse.

At the final stage of life, dissaving for old age care, and transfer to the next generation, as inherence or trusts are common. The curved line show inflow revenues over time, and strait line shows the living costs expenses, or outflows during youth, middle age, and old age life time.

Figure 8 shows cases 1, 2, dissaving, and saving, with costs in life cycles. That is dissaving in youth and old age, and saving when working. Therefore, the static cost line does not show inflation adjustment over time.

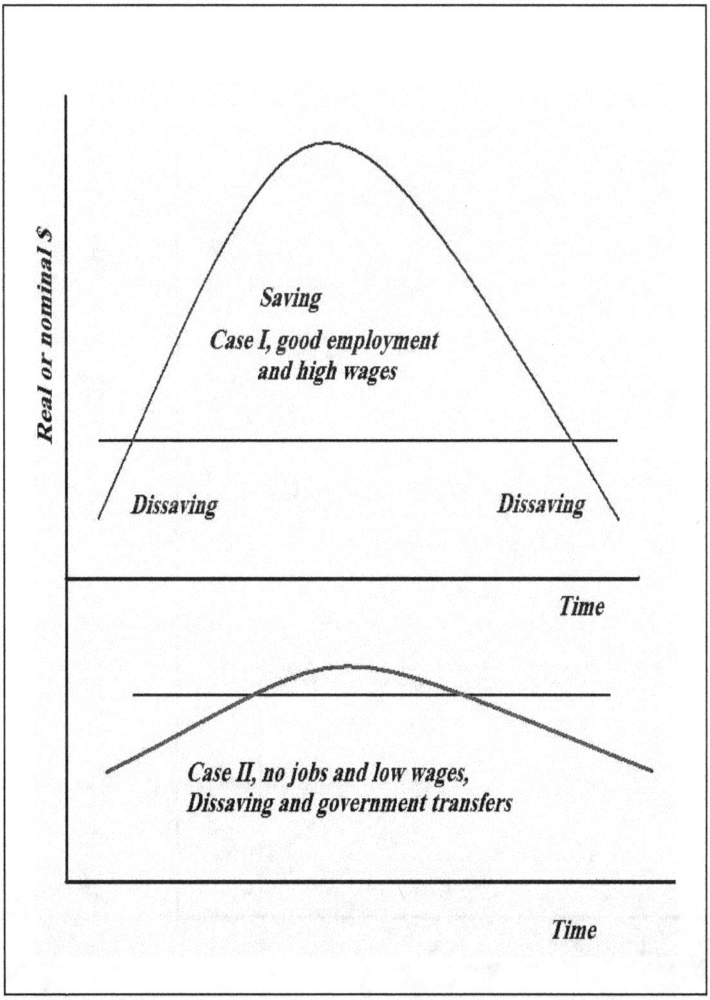

Figure 8, Dissaving, and saving, with costs of life cycles.

Figure 9 shows a new dynamic aspect of inflated higher costs occurring at different stages of the individual life cycles. Thus, the quality, duration, and enumeration (living wages) of employment have to be very good.

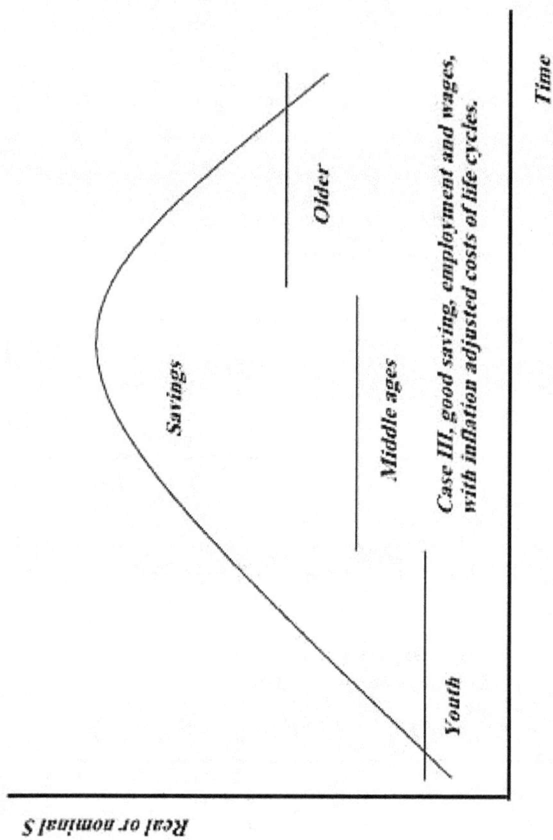

Figure 9, Saving, employment, wages, of life cycles.

These presentations should have fully informed the reader to the premier significance of teconomics of dynamic budgeting at different stage of lifetime operations.

Good dynamic budgeting offers a chance to even mediocre production to survive bad revenue years, when the business cycles turn, from operational advantages of businesses in good business cycle years.

In cases of individuals, government transfers in term of education, retraining, job opportunities, research and development funds, and private in temporal savings will help. Governmental strategies help by infrastructure projects, construction, and job services, which supply survival bridges to times that are more prosperous, and offer poor children and old age protection against destitution, premature and costly sickness, and early death.

It offers a chance to governments in bad economic turn, in cases of severe recessions and depression to structure constructive ways out of misfortunate unemployment and chronic structural underemployment situation.[13] Economic conditions, which do not lend to self-remedy and dreamy cooperate supply-side economic theories of recent varieties. There are no laws against NGO-donor billionaires' generosities. They work wonderfully; except, they can take darker turns, and become self-serving, self-regulatory to lead to wealth concentrations, and worst dictatorial without checks and balances. Another problem occurs when they are help is needed. That is when economies take sharp downturns into depression, and these NGO-donors are economically most constrained, or immobile by risk aversion. Moreover, the tax-revenues funds shortfalls, they have denied the government no longer exists to remedy the downturns by government investment increases. The economic science is not offering the reader dogma here. It strongly suggests that alternatives sources of resources that include the governmental resources are preferable to ideologues exclusions by unintelligible dogmas. Therefore, teconomics of dynamic sustainable budgets offer constructive methodology for advancement.

Notes

[1] Dr. Bahman Fakhraie, Teconomics: the microeconomic analysis, Utah, FERDAT publishing 2012, and, https://www.createspace.com/4196760,

[2] From Latin word bulga, celtic and Middle Irish bolg, or old English belg refer belly, and to bag or purse, French 15th century.
Barnhart, C. L. *The World Book Dictionary*, Chicago, Doubleday & Company, Inc. 1974

[3] The symbol is on clay and on rock pictorials, -550 BC Persia.

[4] Webster's Ninth New Collegiate Dictionary, Springfield, Massachusetts, Merriam-Webster Inc. 1985

[5] Project proposals were presented to NSF 2013. It detailed monetization proposals as large-scale fiscal job creation methodologies.

[6] For Dr. Bahman Fakhraie books and EBooks check the book web page at, http://bahfecon.wix.com/bahfecon

[7] Bahman Fakhraie, PhD. *Teconomics: the microeconomic analysis*, Utah, FERDAT publishing 2012, and, https://www.createspace.com/4196760,

[8] Bahman Fakhraie, PhD. *Technological injection, dynamic new capital measurements, and Production Theory in Economics*, (Michigan: ProQuest LLC, 2010) https://order.proquest.com/OA_HTML/pqdtibeCCtpItmDspRte.jsp
Dr. Bahman Fakhraie's Books web page is at, http://bahfecon.wix.com/bahfecon

[9] Dr. Bahman Fakhraie, *"Treatise on Dynamic Risks, All Disasters, And Energy Resource Production Disasters,"* scientific paper, 10,28, Utah FERDAT Publishing 2013, https://plus.google.com/u/0/?tab=mX#stream/circles/p57ebfa130e9cc418

[10] Hutchinson, Harry D. *Money, Banking, And The United States Economy*, 3rd. ed. New jersey, Englewood Cliffs, Prentice-Hall, Inc.

[11] For an examples for evolution of notes, and T-accounts examples read,
Dr. Bahman Fakhraie, *TECONOMICS OF VERBALISM,* Utah FERDAT Publishing 2012,
ISBN-978-0-9852958-4-4,
https://www.createspace.com/4121720, and
Short, D. G., Welsch, G.A. Fundamentals of Financial Accounting, (Boston MA, IRWIN Inc. 6ed, 1974), 96-99

[12] Ibid, p. 107

[13] Dr. Bahman Fakhraie, *TECONOMICS OF VERBALISM*, Utah FERDAT Publishing 2012,
ISBN-978-0-9852958-4-4,
https://www.createspace.com/4121720

CHPTER 2

The Inflows

The income from individual jobs, plus returns on savings, interest, rent, sales of items, old cars are summed up in this category.

Firms have more detailed itemization, income revenues from all operations, sales, and modular production outputs, goods, and services are accumulated under this heading. Returns from sales of farm products, cash crop, livestock, or dairy products are itemized separately, as grow sales. Sales of salvage of depreciated farm equipment, sales of land parcels, are added in the small firm budgets, too.

The summation of all revenues establishes the revenues for all related operations and household income. Most new family farm and small family businesses, without aid of capable advisors, forget to separate the family budget from the firm's operational budget. That is one of the earliest red flag in most audits.

The inflow Presentation

The first line separation line is routine. However, a systematic presentation can refresh or assist some readers.

Figure 10 shows the target area of the spreadsheet. This portion block of spreadsheet formulations starts at A4 to K4, and ends at to A11to K1.

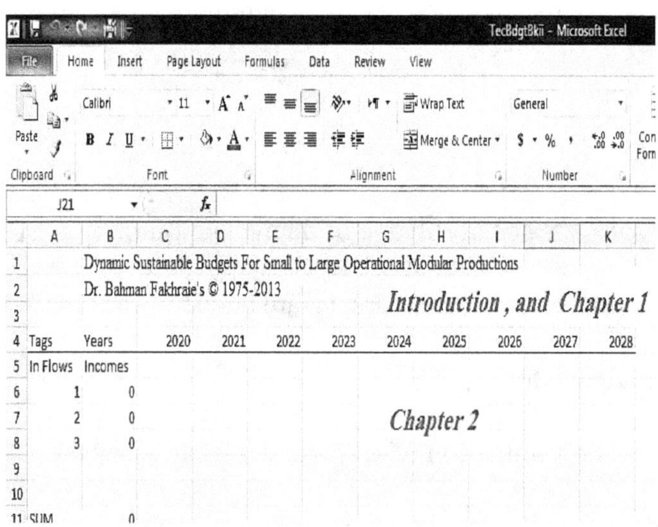

Figure 10, Income inflow portion of the spreadsheet.

The top heading columns of some spreadsheet starts with alphabet, A, B ... AA, ZZ, etc. The rows start with ordinal numbers 1, 2 ... etc. The combination gives you a geographical location on the spreadsheet as a cell. Move the cursor in cell A4, and type Tag, category, Types, Kinds, Years, are written in the same fashion. Thus, we move the cursor, (point, or arrow) over to the next cell B4, and type Years. Table 1 shows the same steps for simple, individual formulations.

Table 2, Create the income flow section on the spreadsheet.

Cell name	Type or Select	Appearance
A4	Tag	the same
C4	2020	The same
D4	=C4+1	2021
Copy> D4 to	F4 to K4	2022-2028
R-click, A4-K4	Bottom Border	line A4-K4
A5	Income Flow	The same
A6	code1, or wages	The same

In the next step we first type the initial year, in this sample is 2020, then we use formula plus copy to finish the line out. The cursor is moved in cell C4, and type 2020. Then, move the cursor to D4, and type the (=C4+1). When you finish click enter button or return. Number 2022 appears in cell E4. Right click cell E4, select copy, and then start the cursor from F4 to K4 and past, numbers 2023 to 2028 will appear, in row 4.

The final touch is also simple. Use the right cursor to select cells A4 to K4 then from the tool diagram on top of the spreadsheet, our from right clicking the mouse you get a tool box, select the window with underlined on it, and not the U, the line appears under all the designated cells.

Itemizing the Inflow Categories

The first add the inflow, income descriptions, the first column is also used to enumerate sources of income. In this sample number codes are used they can represent different jobs, family members' jobs, small business, farm products, cash crops, live stocks, real estate rentals or sales, or interest, and rent, etc. Alternatively, the same items instead of numeral codes can be written in the spreadsheet, followed by their summation at the bottom of the inflow section.

Classifications of Inflows

Simpler budgeting will not need additional steps under this subheading of inflows. The additions of small firm, farms, jobs add to the complexities, therefore, classification will introduce order assuming a few rules are followed,

1. Unified reporting system exists.
2. Inflows are added to a unified cash record.
3. There is a designated record keeper.

Additional sub-title development can help with the record keeping. There are cogent analyses of contemplation about keeping them separate automatically. Therefore, developing separate budgeting for each inflow categories separately. It is fine, as long as, record keeping is good and the records are maintained diligently.

Small Business and Family Income Flow

Table 3 shows more complex income-inflow formulations from sales of different products.

Table 3, Business, and family inflow spreadsheet

Cell name	Type or Select	Appearance
A4	Tag	the same
C4	2020	The same
D4	=C4+1	2021
Copy> D4 to	F4 to K4	2022-2028
R-click, A4-K4	Bottom Border	line A4-K4
A5	Income Flows	The same
A6	code1, or wages	The same
A7	Ag, chicken, eggs	The same
A8	2, hey, grain, beef	The same
A9	3, fruit, jam	The same
A10	pottery, dishes ,art	The same
A11	interest, dividends	The same
A12	Sum	=sum(A6:A12)

Individual and Family Income

Individuals that have more than one job or source of revenue inflows, benefit of ordering them under this sub-heading.

For example, husband's job one is written as, hj1 and job two is hj2. Wife job one is noted as wj1. Children with jobs are added in the same fashion, son job 1 as, sj1, and daughter, as dj1. The children names can be used, too. Retirement benefit from husband old first job is hrb1.

Usual family budgets start and finish about here. Especially, in training children to live their independent lives, they need to understand the principles of budgeting early in their lives habitually. Their own budget plans assist in that endeavor mightily. That has lifecycle positive externalities.

There are more circumstances, when each economic agent or agencies can require a separate budget to detail their specific and more complex itemization. In some cases, using the same budgeting tools may prove to be more difficult, for all involved.

Unified classification will prove less beneficial in some cases,

1. Unified reporting system does not exist.
2. Teach children independent budgeting.
3. Family budget is too complex.
4. Firms' budgets are too complex.

There will also be circumstances, which additional supplementary record keeping, and sophisticated financial advice will be needed. That is even with a unified budgeting in place,

i. Record keeping, prior to budgeting,
ii. Along with budgeting,
iii. In tax preparation,
iv. For tax audits,
v. For managerial audits

Nevertheless, there are complex family budgets, which include trusts and investment returns, inherences settlements, real estate sales, jewelry and artwork sales and more. Moreover, at certain stages, beyond certified public accountants (CPA) employing financial professionals that truly work for your interests can pay some dividends. There are books stating that is increasingly more difficult, among divided interested and divided loyalties to obtain positive and monitored results. The wrong kind of hired help can be very harmful and costly, as well.

Saving and Investment Funds

Once careers are established, individuals quickly understand a few facts. The one fact that stays with workers, or it should stay with them, is the fact that your costs tail your new salary like hands and gloves, regardless how high the income it gets, and your costs do catch with your new incomes, even if you are saving proactively. If you fail to plan a budget, you plan to fail your budget. The saving from your new income vanishes quickly.

Therefore, the straggle to increase your income funds, find good jobs, and other investments to boost your income flow are only part of the life cycle economic story. The formulation of your budget planning will encourage a serious look where your economies are in the larger economy, and how to sustain a balance life for yourselves, importantly.

The next segment, explains how skills and new technological improvements can help your economy. Therefore, dynamic budgeting place.

Technological Injections Stratagems

Saving and investment funds are accumulated and materialize as your budgeting details your income flow, and help constrain your expenses.

The modular production processes, like the origination, circularity, and technological injection of innovation in production have been extensity covered in Dr. Bahman Fakhraie research and books.[1] Here we start in period one (t1), with an initial cash, purchase of inputs, good, services, skills, and a chosen production process, which can be updated by technological injection, at t2 period.

After the production of outputs, of goods and services, they are presented to market for successful sale.[2] After successful sales cash inflows exceed production costs and the expenses, therefore there are surplus funds for saving and investment in period two (t2).

In theoretical economics, we are marginal revenue is exceeding average costs sufficiently to generate profit, and accumulate investment funds in the longer run.

The sustainability matters here, because investment of technological injections and replacement of obsolete methods of modular production is a longer-term proposition, and it requires larger investment funds, both of which require sustained revenues inflows and profitability in the longer run. Therefore, periods t2, and t3 should generate revenues to establish market shares, and in some cases technological and or government-granted monopolistic competitive edge. Those will deliver the sustainable profitability for the modular production in operation. Figure 11 shows dynamic cash flow and surplus from production flow from the transaction process.

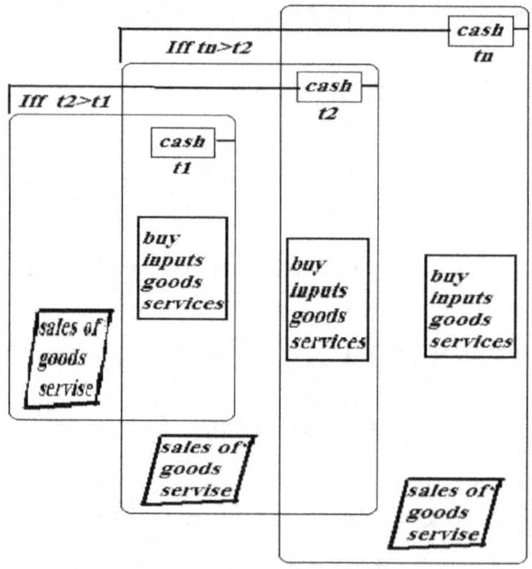

Teconomics of dynamic cash flow of production of goods and services in a growing business with technological injections.

Figure 11, Dynamic cash flow and production surpluses.

Therefore, the strategy of change and growth is a reasonable target for technological injections. Thus, governments can assist and or engage in sequestrations, or deficits-political brawls to a no growth path. That involves private and governmental infrastructure investments, beyond subsidizations of obsolete technologies in place. This is another example of dynamic teconomics of applied technological injections of investment fund accumulated from growing modular-production operation, which uses dynamic budgeting and guards its surplus revenues from sales.[3] This is the most vivid application of Dr. Bahman Fakhraie scholarly work, and books to developmental economics in modern applied economics.

Notes

[1] Dr. Bahman Fakhraie, *TECONOMICS*, Utah FERDAT Publishing 2012,
ISBN/EAN13: 0985295813 / 9780985295813,
https://www.createspace.com/4196760

[2] Bahman Fakhraie, PhD, *DEMAND AND SUPPLY SIDES OF TECHNOLOGICAL INJECTIONS*,
ISBN-978-0-9852958-3-7,
http://www.amazon.com/Demand-supply-Sides-Technological-Injections/dp/098529583X/ref=sr_1_4?ie=UTF8&qid=1360206619&sr=8-4&keywords=BAHMAN+FAKHRAIE,
or http://bahfecon.wix.com/bahfecon

[3] Bahman Fakhraie, PhD., *Technological injection, dynamic new capital measurements, and Production Theory in Economics*, (Michigan: ProQuest LLC, 2010),
https://order.proquest.com/OA_HTML/pqdtibeCCtpItmDspRte.jsp
Dr. Bahman Fakhraie Books web page is at,
http://bahfecon.wix.com/bahfecon

CHPTER 3

The Outflows

The outflows are accumulated costs of operations. They are the dynamic variable costs, the flex cost of operations, and outflows of cash for fixed cost utilities, daily operation and expenses, which occur and are due during the establishment and operation of processes related to households and modular production activities.

For the introductory and elemental introductions, we will start with figure 12. However, the out flow of households and even small businesses and farming operations can get very complex; use of professionals, libraries, books, training and studies is advised.

Figure 12 shows the outflows portion of the spreadsheet.

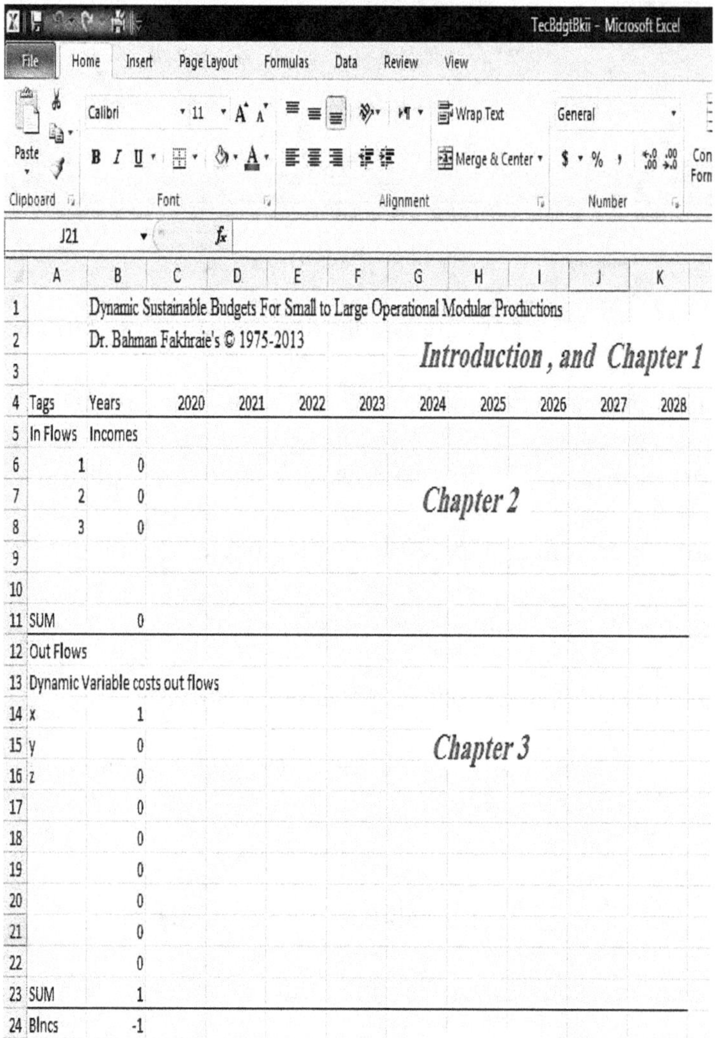

	A	B	C	D	E	F	G	H	I	J	K
1		Dynamic Sustainable Budgets For Small to Large Operational Modular Productions									
2		Dr. Bahman Fakhraie's © 1975-2013					Introduction, and Chapter 1				
3											
4	Tags	Years	2020	2021	2022	2023	2024	2025	2026	2027	2028
5	In Flows	Incomes									
6	1	0									
7	2	0					Chapter 2				
8	3	0									
9											
10											
11	SUM	0									
12	Out Flows										
13	Dynamic Variable costs out flows										
14	x	1									
15	y	0						Chapter 3			
16	z	0									
17		0									
18		0									
19		0									
20		0									
21		0									
22		0									
23	SUM	1									
24	Blncs	-1									

Figure 12, Outflows portion of the spreadsheet.

Table 4 show formulations and spreadsheet cells presentation for the outflows.

Table 4, Inflow formulation.

Cell name	Type or Select	Appearance
A12	Outflows	the same
A13	Dynamic costs	The same
A14	X	The same
A15	Y	The same
A16	Z	The same
...	...	...
A23	Sum	=Sum(A15:A23)
A24	H>bottom border	--------------
A25	Balance	The same
A25	=A14-A24	The same

Classifications of outflows

The classification of numbers of items and products, which the consumers spend money on are important parts of the record keeping.

The temporal elements that make the budget design dynamic include inflationary (COLA, price based) adjustment.

The sustainability conditions are at play for maintenances of items, and application of capital project funds. These will make certain that elemental modular operations and productions are fully functional.

Technological injections will improve the modular production, and they will give the holistic production project longevity as well. They apply other important contributory parts to sustainability, too.

Individual and Family Outflows

Fixed costs are costs that are paid regularly, monthly, and they are paid first. The flex, or variable cost items, as the households' items, are less rigid expenditures. Their quality or quantity modify at harder times, when consumer income may be more constrained. The lists of these items are as follows,

Taxes,

Federal, States, Localities, Real estate

Legal Costs

Utilities,

Phones, Gas, Electrical

Rental Costs,

Auto costs

Auto loans, Maintenances, Petrol

Flex costs,

Credit cards,

Loans

Households' costs

Food

Cloth

Education,

Restaurant, movies

Reading and fun

/Sum

/Balance of Small Business and Family Operations,

Inflow and Outflows

For business and households, we add the following to households' items,

Real Estate

Households' costs

Agricultural operations, Ag costs, Farm Operations,

Orchards, fruits, jam and preserve, dry fruits,

Grains, Hey, dairy operation, milk, cheese, fertilize,

Range cattle, beef, and calf, meat, fertilizer,

Sheep, goats, milk, cheese, meat, fertilizer,

Chicken, eggs, meat, fertilizer,

Handicrafts, woodworking & toys, writing,

In table 5, and figure 13, the combined efforts of inflow and outflow sales and costs are presented. The combinations should aid the student with demonstrated example, which help write spreadsheets that are more complex.

In table 5, the cell names, we have included cell row and column designations, plus identity or cell name. For example A9, fruit sales. Arithmetic or statistical formulas are proceeded with (=) sign. They are placed under type, or select columns. What appears in the cells is indicated in the appurtenance column. Figure 13 shows the result in excel spreadsheet. Multiple pages are used to calculate separate record keeping associated with different modular operations. In this example, only the fruit sales and costs are calculated under the sheet name fruits. The two sheets framed from cut and pastes in a one page graphic form. The same multiple arrangements and presentations are made for range cattle, diary, sheep, goats, chickens, and poultry, or dry farming, handicraft, woodshop, and other small modular productions, under different name tags. Table 5 shows inflow, outflow formulations from multiple sheets. Figure 13 shows inflow, outflow formulations from multiple related sheets.

Table 5, Inflows and outflows from multiple sheets.

Cell name	Type or Select	Appearance
A4	Tag	the same
C4	2020	The same
D4	=C4+1	2021
Copy> D4 to	F4 to K4	2022-2028
R-click A4-K4	Bottom Border	line A4-K4
A5	Income Flows	The same
A6	code1. or wages	The same
A7	Ag, chicken, eggs	The same
A8	2, hey, grain, beef	The same
A9 fruit sales	=sum(fruits!B3:B6)	650
A12	Out Flows	The same
A17	Farm Ops	The same
A24 fruits,	=sum(fruits!B12:B25)	550
A34 SUM	=SUM(B35:B36)	552
A35Profitblnc	=B11-B34	98

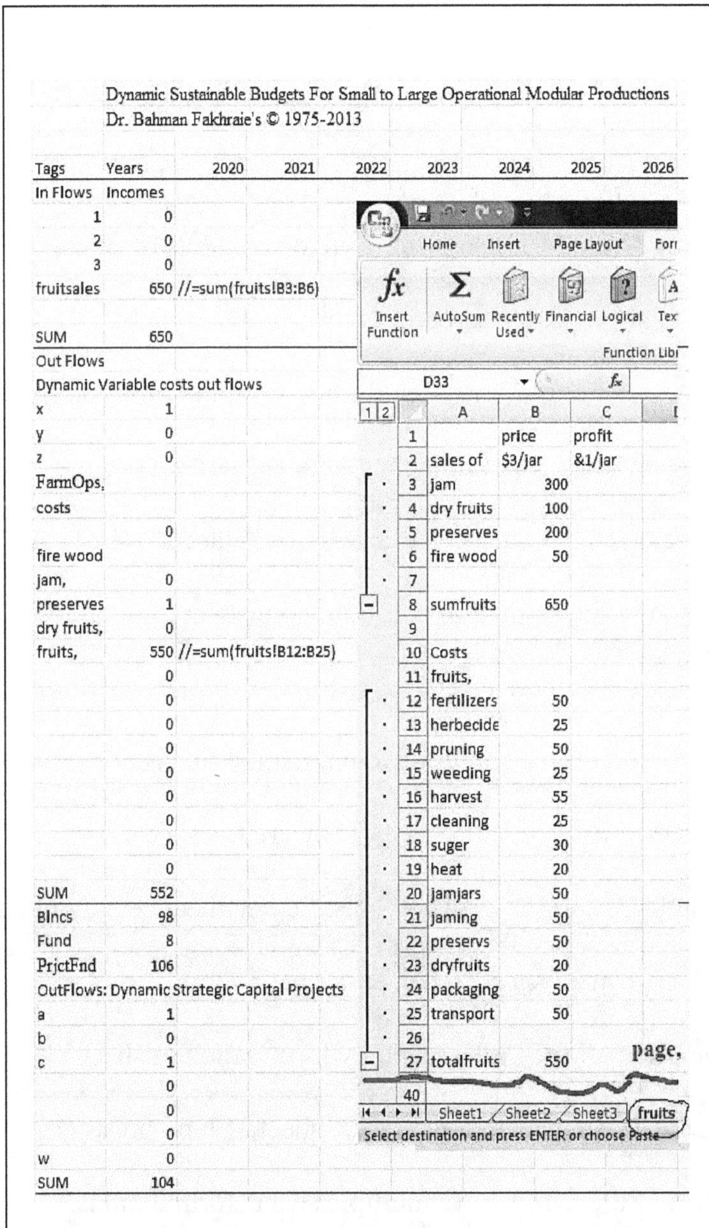

Figure 13, Inflow, outflow formulations on multiple sheets.

In table 5, A9 fruit sales, =sum (fruits!B3:B6), 650 detail the formulation of multiple sheet data used in one main sheet 1. That is in cell A9, the formulation written in "=sum (fruits! B3:B6)" sums up the contents of cells B3 to B6, in sheet 'fruits' and copies them in the designated cell in sheet 1. The figure 13, details, and formulation of multiple sheet uses are denoted again. Another method is to go in the selected cell in sheet 1, and write "=Jam!B29". That will copy the content of cell B29 from sheet Jam in the designated cell on sheet 1.

Figure 14 shows different named sheets related and compiled in sheet number 1. They are the sheets named Jam, fruits, preserve. Their specific details are enumerated in their named sheet. Then either their summations are compiled, or they are copied by formulation in sheet 1. Figure 14 shows the four sheets, sheet 1, Jam, preserve, fruits. Figure 14 shows multiple sheets formulations.

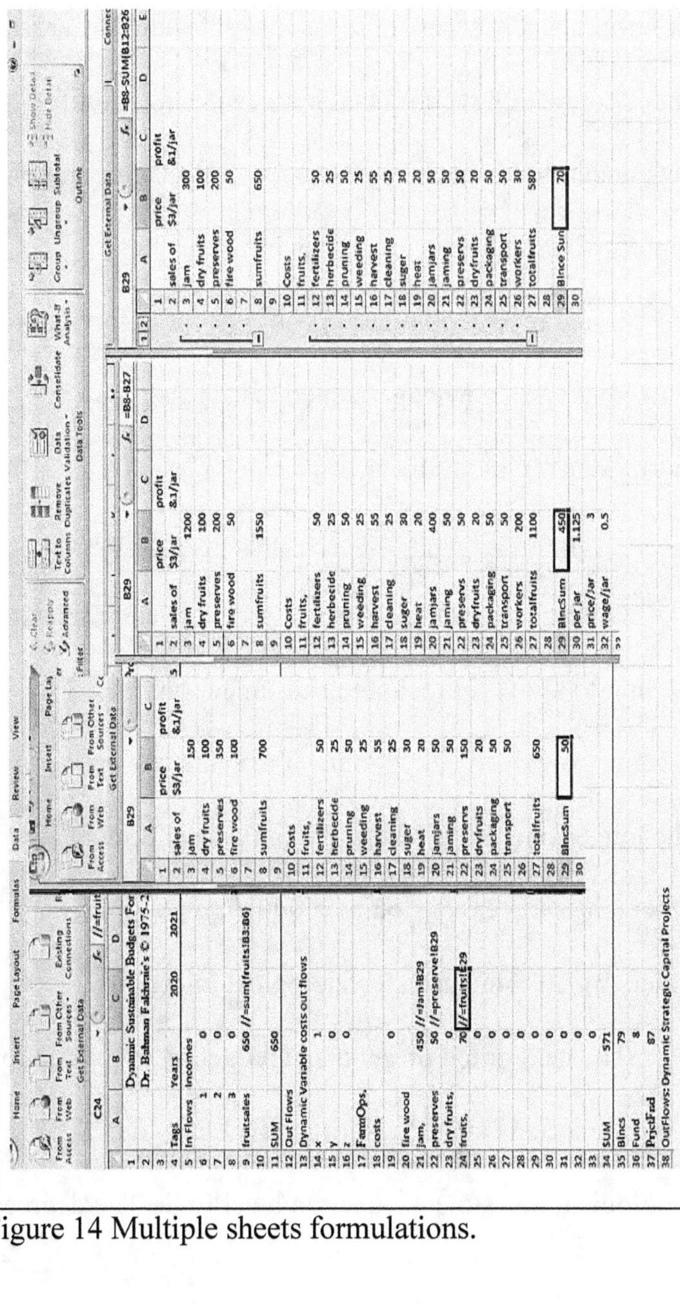

Figure 14 Multiple sheets formulations.

These show the reader how more complex spreadsheets with multi-sheet nesting are formed from small businesses to more complex governmental budgets, using multiple sheets under different titles to separate modular operations distinctly. Nevertheless, many governments have demonstrated repeatedly that it is not just the information but the skill and knowledge, which distinguish the importance of final products.

Temporal Economic Advancement Policy

Once again, we use the two period t1 and t2, budget modeling to allow for technological injections and economic growth and development to shape the economy in the longer run. In this case, dynamic cash flow of last chapter is used in expansion of production possibility frontiers by investment in technological injections.

The next graph presents the reduction in production and consumptions and equilibrium level Et1, to the post-technological investment-injection level Epd. The degrees of recovery will depend on both private free market, and governmental (national and international trainings, aids, trades), producers, individuals in the less developed zone (LDZ) will receive in exchanges, in order, to make them better off at E1, at t2 time.

That is sometime in the future, which will be a lost. In the other hand, private markets can help with recovery loans, and technological assists, which will advance the individuals to their higher social welfare position at E2 equilibriums, unless imperfect (political and economic) markets conditions persists.[1]

At each level, E2, Et1, E1, Epd signify these different levels of production and consumptions. The temporal consumption adjustment allows for paying interest of the loans (from E1, to Epd), until enhance trade advances enables the full payoffs and advancement to Et1, and with trade to E2.

Figure 14 shows temporal technological injections possible due to proper budgeting.

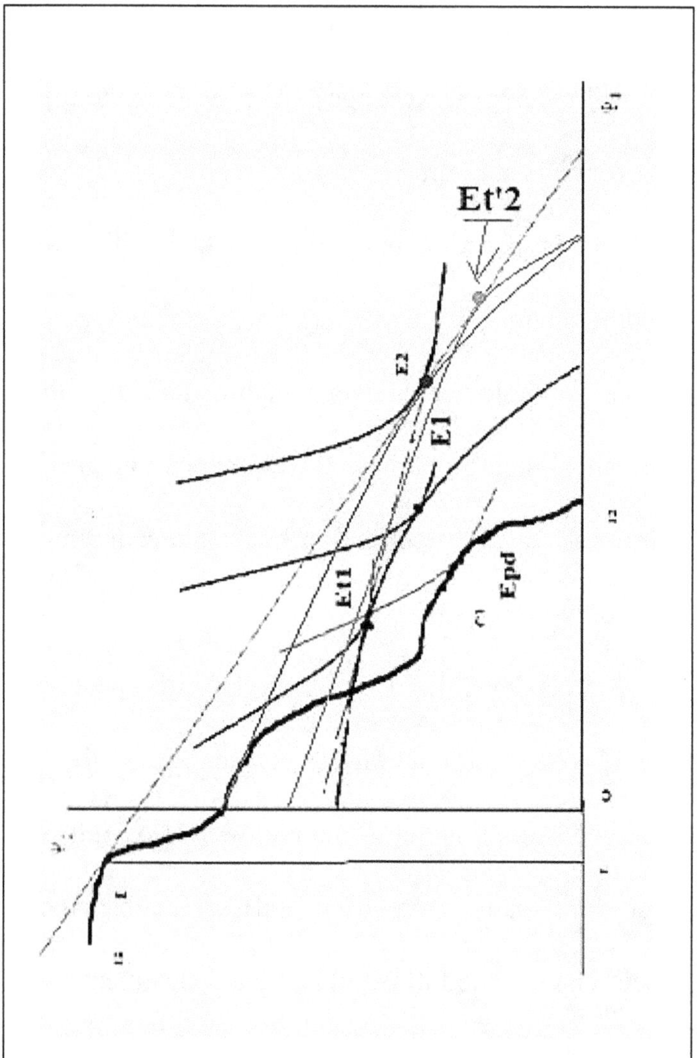

Figure 15, Temporal technological injections.

Figure 14 allows for post investment modular production adjustments, after initial loans are reinvested in technological injections to improve production possibilities and enhance benefits from global trade.[2] The technological injections will increase production possibilities to the other curve and E't2 level, if the advantages of the global trade in a two nation model are not fully realized. The mixed combination of bundle of goods and services (q1, q2) at E2 is assumed of higher utilities to the (q'1, q'2) at Et'2. That is the main reason both countries and economies engage in the trade, to be both at a better position than without the trade, with a higher mix of goods and services.

There are going to be naked aggression against the technological inevitability and the evolution of modular production practices and policies. Competitors and their paid political helps will countermand well. Most attempts and theological counter culture wars to hold back progress will again fail, as they often have failed.

On the other hand, misapplications of technological innovation to spy, monitor, and holdback employments, dissent, living salaries, and marketable resources, capital, labors' skills, natural resources, from free markets also exists. These inflect inequities, imbalances, and unsustainable conditions in welfare theory.[3] Yet, there are equitable exchanges and redistribution of global wealth creation, and appropriate trades and global commerce, which are still practiced. They are sustained eventually.

That is different from wealth miss-concentrations and harmful past wealth-concentrations in international unsuitable trades. These models will also come to the dead-end results that other recursive confiscatory policies have reached. Humanity is not able to kill its way to halting human progress toward improvements of humanities' condition. The extended human history attests to such continuum.

Notes

[1] Dr. Bahman Fakhraie, *TECONOMICS*, Utah FERDAT Publishing 2012,
ISBN/EAN13: 0985295813 / 9780985295813,
https://www.createspace.com/4196760

[2] Bahman Fakhraie, PhD., Technological injection, dynamic new capital measurements, and Production Theory in Economics, (Michigan: ProQuest LLC, 2010),
https://order.proquest.com/OA_HTML/pqdtibeCCtpItmDspRte.jsp

[3] Dr. Bahman Fakhraie, TECONOMICS, Utah FERDAT Publishing 2012,
ISBN/EAN13: 0985295813 / 9780985295813,
https://www.createspace.com/4196760

CHPTER 4

Sustainable Modular Productions Budgets

Conducting a budget plan seem the simplest of tasks. However, as in production there are elemental parts that make the holistic sum functional and relevant.[1] They add to the complexities of production processes.

The formulation for nesting, and coping from different sheets to organize the final budget were presented. The bold numbers are presented as the elements of current maintenance items, which are required to be paid monthly for the operational maintenances of all modular productions that make the holistic project function regularly. There are some elements, like taxes that have to be saved monthly, and then paid annually, when they are required to be paid. Figure 16 shows the sustainable modular production budget.

D37 | =SUM(D10:D36)

	A	B / C	D	E	F	G	H	I	J	K	L
1		Dr. Bahman Fakhraie's ® 1975-2013 ,									
2		All development and legal rights are reserved to Dr. Bahman Fakhraie									
3		**Years**	**20 13/14**	**2014/15**	**2115/16**	**2016/17**	**?1017/18**	**2018/19**	**2019/20**	**2020/21**	**2021/22**
4		unitfee	**230**	**230**	**230**	**230**	**230**	**230**	**230**	**230**	**230**
5		annual	121440	121440	121440	121440	121440	121440	121440	121440	121440
6		bnkblnc21313	33000	58610	71730	68360.9	47766.6	40706.75	9218.882	24776.04	49774.79
7		Refunds,insu,fines									
8		sum inflow	154440	180050	193170	189801	169207	162146.8	130658.9	146216	171214.79
9		**Categories**									
10		Snow		**0**	**0**	**0**	**0**	**0**	**0**	**0**	**0**
11		Lawn,snow		**0**	**0**	**0**	**0**	**0**	**0**	**0**	**0**
12		Remove,S		**0**	**0**	**0**	**0**	**0**	**0**	**0**	**0**
13		General G		**0**	**0**	**0**	**0**	**0**	**0**	**0**	**0**
14		**Grounds**	**18370**	**19013**	**19678**	**20367**	**21080**	**21817.8**	**22581.4**	**23372**	**24189.78**
15		Water,Sewer		**0**	**0**	**0**	**0**	**0**	**0**	**0**	**0.00**
16		Trash		**0**	**0**	**0**	**0**	**0**	**0**	**0**	**0.00**
17		Natural Gas		**0**	**0**	**0**	**0**	**0**	**0**	**0**	**0.00**
18		Electricity		**0**	**0**	**0**	**0**	**0**	**0**	**0**	**0.00**
19		ClubH,Gates,Phone		**0**	**0**	**0**	**0**	**0**	**0**	**0**	**0.00**
20		**Utilities**	**44823**	**46392**	**48016**	**49696**	**51435**	**53235.7**	**55098.9**	**57027**	**59023.33**
21				**0**	**0**	**0**	**0**	**0**	**0**	**0**	**0.00**
22		Insurance		**0**	**0**	**0**	**0**	**0**	**0**	**0**	**0.00**
23		Legals,banks		**0**	**0**	**0**	**0**	**0**	**0**	**0**	**0.00**
24		Tax, Fed		**0**	**0**	**0**	**0**	**0**	**0**	**0**	**0.00**
25		Tax, Property		**0**	**0**	**0**	**0**	**0**	**0**	**0**	**0.00**
26		**Legal,Ins,Tax**	**3187**	**3299**	**3414**	**3533**	**3657**	**3785.16**	**3917.64**	**4054.8**	**4196.67**
27				**0**	**0**	**0**	**0**	**0**	**0**	**0**	**0.00**
28		Repairs, Suppl, pool		**0**	**0**	**0**	**0**	**0**	**0**	**0**	**0.00**
29		Buiding mntnc		**0**	**0**	**0**	**0**	**0**	**0**	**0**	**0.00**
30		pool/ClubH		**0**	**0**	**0**	**0**	**0**	**0**	**0**	**0.00**
31		**Repairs,Suppli**	**4341**	**4493**	**4650**	**4813**	**4981**	**5155.75**	**5336.2**	**5523**	**5716.27**
32				**0**	**0**	**0**	**0**	**0**	**0**	**0**	**0.00**
33		Office Supplies		**0**	**0**	**0**	**0**	**0**	**0**	**0**	**0.00**
34		Socials		**0**	**0**	**0**	**0**	**0**	**0**	**0**	**0.00**
35		**Supplies**	**365**	**377.8**	**391**	**404.7**	**418.8**	**433.506**	**448.678**	**464.38**	**480.64**
36				**0**	**0**	**0**	**0**	**0**	**0**	**0**	**0.00**
37		**Sum Flex**	**71086**	**73574**	**76149**	**78814**	**81573**	**84428**	**87383**	**90441**	**93607**
38		**blncoppr inflo**	83354	106476	117021	110987	87633.8	77718.88	43276.04	55774.79	77608.107
39		**Projects**		0		0	0	0	0	0	0
40		ClubH	0	0	8000	0	0	7000	0	0	0
41		Paint ext	0	0	0	0	35000	35000	0	0	0
42		Gutters	2500	0	0	0	0	23000			0
43		Patios,sidewalks	1050	3500	3500	0	0	3500	3500	3500	3500
44		Paving E/W	10394	0	0	5000	11927	0	0		6146
45		Roofs		29446	34360	58220	0	0	0	0	0
46	added	Balconies	1800	1800	1800	0	0	0	0	0	0
47		Pool	9000	0	1000	0	0	0	5000	2500	2500
48		Tennis	0	0	0	0	0	0	10000	0	0
49		sumfix	24744	34746	48660	63220	46927	68500	18500	6000	12146
50		**GrandTotal"**	58610	71730	68361	47766.6	40706.8	9218.882	24776.04	49774.79	65462.107
51				0	0	0	0	0	0	0	0
52		**Sum Totals**	95830	108320	124809	142034	128500	152927.9	105882.8	96441.24	105752.69
53				0	0	0	0	0	0	0	0
54		BlncChecking 6/29/12		0	0	0	0	0	0	0	0
55		BlncProjects 6/29/12		0	0	0	0	0	0	0	0
56		Total Blnc		0	0	0	0	0	0	0	0
57		ForwardBlnc		0	0	0	0	0	0	0	0
58											
59		Actualdatablnc	**58610**	**71730**	**68361**	**47767**	**40707**	**9219**	**24776**	**49775**	**65462**

Figure 16, The sustainable modular production budget.

The elements are bid separately. Hired maintenance professionals can handle them, too. However, since each item adds to the holistic sum, costs and final expenses dictate frugality and careful handling of the budget items. Sometime, volunteerism can save portion of the costs, too. Experienced and skilled managers utilize all available resources.

Modular Parts of the Holistic Production Budget

This example of multiple acreages condominium project shows us the modular parts that have to be budgeted on different sheet or separately and then added up to determine the final total budget. The summations of all these modular operations lead to the final operational success of the holistic operational production model.

The significances exceed parochial views as technological leaps scribe it. Government funded initial mega-projects do not show the holistic externalities of their operation lifecycles. They will also have circular flow and distributive implication to sustain the economic activities, and encourage economic growth in line with the natural rate of economic growth, in order, to avoided excessive recessionary recurrences.

However, it will be a mistake to assume, their numerous potential profitable and commercial offshoots can be contained. The positive externalities associated with such technological injections will permeate and benefit the free markets locally, regionally, or even globally.[2] Nevertheless, there will also be negative externalities and developing costs, as technological injection break new grounds.[3] Negative externalities costs can be new pollutions, or side effects of the new approaches. Therefore, they will need new science-developments to countermand their evolving new effects and accumulative cots, overtime.

The processes are not static occurrences, and onetime events. The theoretical interrelationship of dynamic budgets and modular productions are developed and further explained as economic theory for equilibrium conditions in the next chapters.

Notes

[1] John A. Hopkin, Ph.D. Peter j. Barry, Ph.D., C.B. Baker, Ph.D. *Finical Management In Agriculture*, (Danville, Illinois: the Interstates Printers & Publishers, Inc.

[2] Bahman Fakhraie, PhD. *TECONOMICS OF VERBALISM*, Utah FERDAT Publishing 2012, ISBN-978-0-9852958-4-4, https://www.createspace.com/4121720

[3] Dr. Bahman Fakhraie, *Teconomic Analysis of Cascading Millennial Economies, Utah FERDAT Publishing 2012,* ISBN-97809852968, ttps://www.createspace.com/4187823

CHPTER 5

Capital Budget, Maintenance Projects Budget

This is the first of two segments on capital budgets. This segment studies the projects maintenance of portion of the budget, the saved amount, which will be contracted out to keep a project, a factory functional, operational, and safe to conduct their daily operational affairs related to modular production. In our example, we are using a hypothetical condominium project, which needs periodical investments to keep its appearance good, and its operations fully functional. Price, marginal revenue, short, and long run average costs are equal. The detailed mathematical presentation and lemmas are in the index section of this book.

Figure 17 shows equilibrium of short and long run costs and prices.

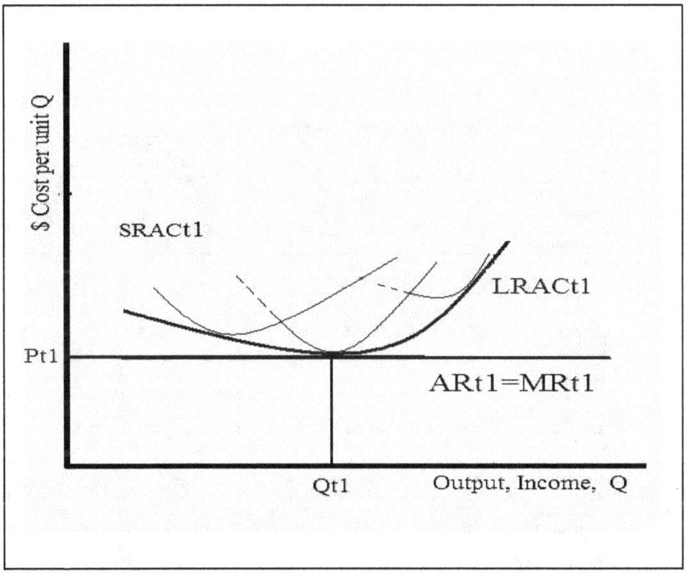

Figure 17, equilibrium of short and long run costs and prices.

Prices must change substantially from Pt1, before temporal technological injections and new capital improvements investment in new modular production are justifiably encouraged.[1] The long run average cost curve is a u-shaped envelope of a series of short run average costs curves. LAC decreases as size of the firm increases, showing efficiency in larger scales, before Q.[2] Then LAC is increasing after Q designating inefficiency.

Figure 18 shows Capital maintenances budget.

B18 fx Water,Sewer

	A	B / C	D	E	F	G	H	I	J	K	L
4		Dr. Bahman Fakhraie's ® 1975-2013 ,									
5		All development and legal rights are reserved to Dr. Bahman Fakhraie									
6		**Years**	**20 13/14**	**2014/15**	**2115/16**	**2016/17**	**21017/18**	**2018/19**	**2019/20**	**2020/21**	**2021/22**
7		unitfee	**230**	**230**	**230**	**230**	**230**	**230**	**230**	**230**	**230**
8		annual	121440	121440	121440	121440	121440	121440	121440	121440	121440
9		bnkblnc21313	33000	58610	71730	68360.9	47766.6	40706.75	9218.88	24776	49774.79
10		Refunds,insu,fines									
11		sum inflow	154440	180050	193170	189801	169207	162146.8	130659	146216	171214.79
12		**Categories**									
13		Snow		0	0	0	0	0	0	0	0
14		Lawn,snow		0	0	0	0	0	0	0	0
15		Remove,S		0	0	0	0	0	0	0	0
16		General G		0	0	0	0	0	0	0	0
17		**Grounds**	18370	19013	19678.4	20367.1	21080	21817.8	22581.4	23371.8	24189.78
18		Water,Sewer		0	0	0	0	0	0	0	0.00
19		Trash		0	0	0	0	0	0	0	0.00
20		Natural Gas		0	0	0	0	0	0	0	0.00
21		Electricity		0	0	0	0	0	0	0	0.00
22		ClubH,Gates,Phone		0	0	0	0	0	0	0	0.00
23		**Utilities**	44823	46392	48015.5	49696.1	51435.4	53235.66	55098.9	57027.4	59023.33
24				0	0	0	0	0	0	0	0.00
25		Insurance		0	0	0	0	0	0	0	0.00
26		Legals,banks		0	0	0	0	0	0	0	0.00
27		Tax, Fed		0	0	0	0	0	0	0	0.00
28		Tax, Property		0	0	0	0	0	0	0	0.00
29		**Legal,Ins,Tax**	3187	3298.5	3413.99	3533.48	3657.16	3785.156	3917.64	4054.75	4196.67
30				0	0	0	0	0	0	0	0.00
31		Repairs, Suppl, pool		0	0	0	0	0	0	0	0.00
32		Buiding mntnc		0	0	0	0	0	0	0	0.00
33		pool/ClubH		0	0	0	0	0	0	0	0.00
34		**Repairs,Suppli**	4341	4492.9	4650.19	4812.94	4981.4	5155.746	5336.2	5522.96	5716.27
35				0	0	0	0	0	0	0	0.00
36		Office Supplies		0	0	0	0	0	0	0	0.00
37		Socials		0	0	0	0	0	0	0	0.00
38		**Supplies**	365	377.78	390.997	404.682	418.846	433.5055	448.678	464.382	480.64
39				0	0	0	0	0	0	0	0.00
40		**Sum Flex**	71086	#####	76149.10	78814.32	81572.82	84427.87	87382.84	90441.24	93606.69
41		**blncoppr inflo**	83354	106476	117021	110987	87633.8	77718.88	43276	55774.8	77608.107
42		**Projects**		**0**		**0**	**0**	**0**	**0**	**0**	**0**
43		ClubH	**0**	**0**	**8000**	**0**	**0**	**7000**	**0**	**0**	**0**
44		Paint ext	**0**	**0**	**0**	**0**	**35000**	**35000**	**0**	**0**	**0**
45		Gutters	**2500**	**0**	**0**	**0**	**0**	**23000**			**0**
46		Patios,sidewalks	**1050**	**3500**	**3500**	**0**	**0**	**3500**	**3500**	**3500**	**3500**
47		Paving E/W	**10394**	**0**	**0**	**5000**	**11927**	**0**	**0**		**6146**
48		Roofs		**29446**	**34360**	**58220**	**0**	**0**	**0**	**0**	**0**
49	added	Balconies	**1800**	**1800**	**1800**	**0**	**0**	**0**	**0**	**0**	**0**
50		Pool	**9000**	**0**	**1000**	**0**	**0**	**0**	**5000**	**2500**	**2500**
51		Tennis	**0**	**0**	**0**	**0**	**0**	**0**	**10000**	**0**	**0**
52		sumfix	**24744**	**34746**	**48660**	**63220**	**46927**	**68500**	**18500**	**6000**	**12146**
53		**GrandTotal"**	58610	71730	68360.9	47766.6	40706.8	9218.882	24776	49774.8	65462.107
54				0	0	0	0	0	0	0	0
55		**Sum Totals**	95830	108320	124809	142034	128500	152927.9	105883	96441.2	105752.69
56				0	0	0	0	0	0	0	0
57		BlncChecking 6/29/12		0	0	0	0	0	0	0	0
58		BlncProjects 6/29/12		0	0	0	0	0	0	0	0
59		Total Blnc		0	0	0	0	0	0	0	0
60		ForwardBlnc		0	0	0	0	0	0	0	0
61											
62		Actualdatablnc	**58610**	**71730**	**68361**	**47767**	**40707**	**9219**	**24776**	**49775**	**65462**

Figure 18, Capital maintenances budget.

Division, specialization, and retraining of workers (human capital), technological improvements, form the economics of scale factors that decrease costs.

Dynamic Maintenances Project Budget

The onetime capital charges for maintenance occur periodically. Therefore, they have to be budgeted periodically. However, the expenditure cannot yield to zero or negative grand total, or zero balance forward to the next periods. That will exceed the set per unit fee charges.

Therefore, these meet the short and long run equilibrium condition, were optimizations conditions and mathematical equilibrium conditions are in agreements.[3] That is, the market driven equilibriums of the short and long run average costs, average revenue and marginal revenue, and price are reaching equilibrium levels. These will hold conditionally true for a period of time, as market organization are favoring relative competitive, or perfectly competitive conditions.

There are periodical adjustments to the units set fees, as inflationary adjustments affect the modular operations' costs. In figure 18, these show in cells, D7 to L7. The inflated costs are also passing from the contractors and utility corporations to the complex modular production.

Notes

[1] Leftwich, R.H., *The Price System and Resource Allocation*, New York, Rinehart & Company, Inc. 1955

[2] John A. Hopkin, Ph.D. Peter j. Barry, Ph.D., C.B. Baker, Ph.D., Finical Management In Agriculture, (Danville, Illinois: the Interstates Printers & Publishers, Inc.

[3] Bahman Fakhraie, PhD., *TECONOMICS*, Utah FERDAT Publishing 2012,
ISBN/EAN13: 0985295813 / 9780985295813,
https://www.createspace.com/4196760

CHPTER 6

Capital Budget, Upgrades, Technological Injections

Technological injections can also assist to undo a lot of the harm, as well. If we allow scientific evaluations and established assumptive exchange, guideposts get to the modular production level and consumers. The size of such a project and its colossal significances as a technological leap scribes it as a government funded initial mega projects, which will contribute greatly to the rise of western industrial advancements, for example USA 1950-1970s.

Figure 19 shows temporal equilibrium of short and long run costs and prices after investments are made. Figure 20 shows the progression from production possibility curves for Q, g, to short, and long run supply and demand curve for Q.

Table 6 shows the decision matrix about types of agriculture capital for time and usage.[1]

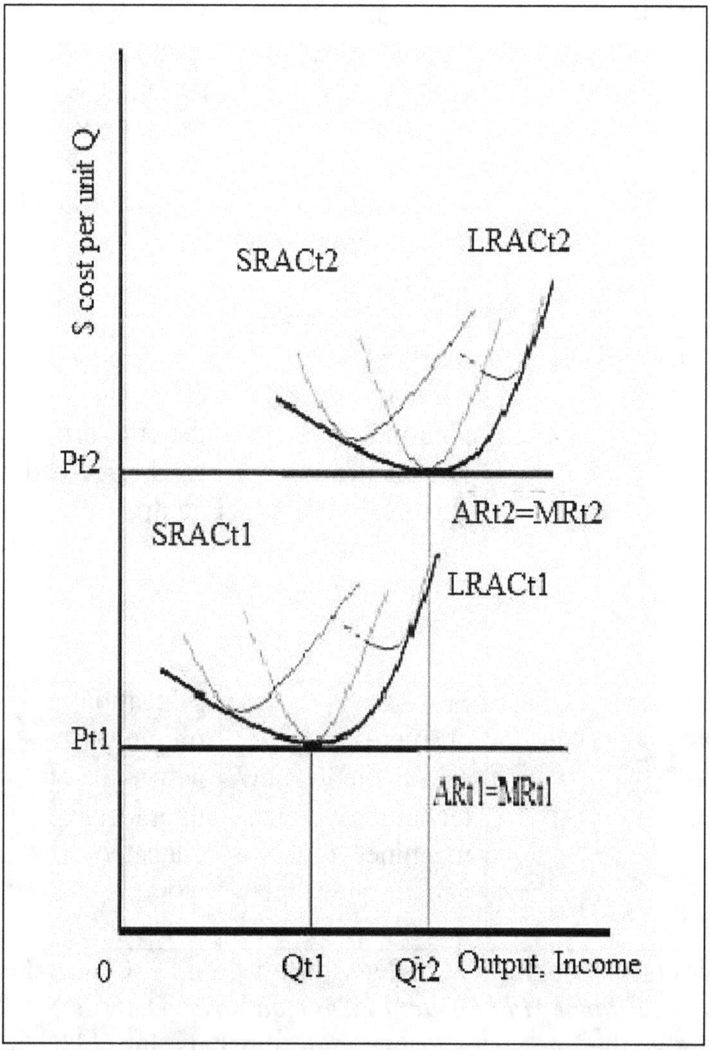

Figure 19, Temporal equilibrium of costs and prices.

Table 6, Decision matrix for types of Agriculture capital.

Time	Capital usage	
	Dedicated capital	General capital
Time fixed capital	Depreciation, taxes, interests, insurance on crop-specific harvester machinery, storage property, seeds in ground fertilizers and chemicals applied	Interest, taxes, land costs, tractors and general use machinery, trucks, other overheads
Time variable capital	Seed before purchase or planting, fertilizers and chemical before application, workers, land rents	Fuels, general chemicals, general farm workers, weed control
Temporal capital & Technological Injections	Entropy or obsolete replacements, new technology crops, machines, tools, genetic seeds, new factory	Education, training, new skill sets, upgrades, educated workers

1-John A. Hopkin, Ph.D., Peter j. Barry, Ph.D., C.B. Baker, Ph.D., *Finical Management In Agriculture,*(Danville, Illinois: the Interstates Printers & Publishers, Inc.,131
2-Authors' addition and upgrades.

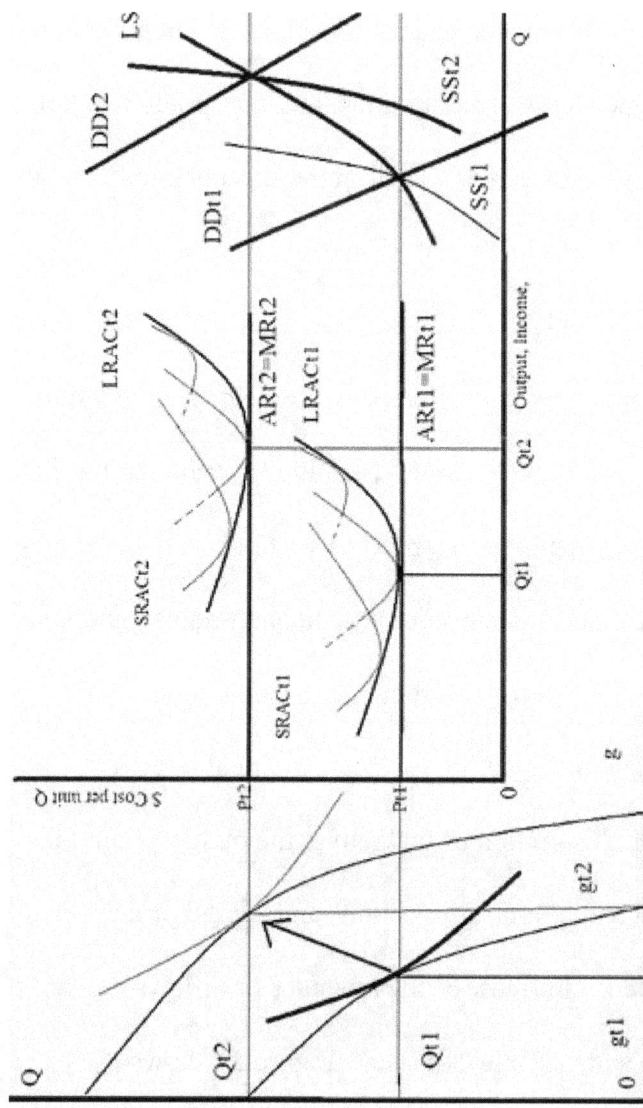

Figure 20 . From PPF tec-expansion to short and long run supply and demand for O

Prices must change substantially from Pt1 to Pt2, before temporal technological injections and new capital improvements investment in new modular production are justifiably encouraged.[2] Their numerous potential profitable and commercial offshoots will benefit the economy holistically. The positive externalities associated with technological injections will permeate and benefit the free markets globally, where permitted.[3] While initial price and revenue increase in a product will induce demand and tec-expansions.[4] The wages and incomes adjustment in a functional economy will soon share the bounty.

Capital Budgeting for Technological Injections

In this section of budgeting, the budget about the temporal technological injections and capital projects is formulated.[5] In figure 3, the revenues or inflows was spent on fixed and variable expenses. Figure 21 shows the capital budget for technological injections, which is forwarded dynamically.

Actuals account balances, main categories 2011-2012

	A	B / C	D	E	F	G	H	I	J	K	L
5		unitfee	230	230	230	230	230	230	230	230	230
6		annual	121440	121440	121440	121440	121440	121440	121440	121440	121440
7	29000	bnkblnc21313	29000	54610	67730	64361	8767	1707	28219	43776	45775
8		Refunds,insu,fines									
9		suminflow	150440	176050	183170	185800.9	130206.57	123146.751	149658.9	165216	167214.79
10		**Categories**	estl#s/Yr	**2015**	**2016**	**2017**	**2018**	**2019**	**2020**	**2021**	**2022**
11		Snow		0	0	0	0	0	0	0	0
12		Lawn,snow		0	0	0	0	0	0	0	0
13		Remove,S		0	0	0	0	0	0	0	0
14		General G		0	0	0	0	0	0	0	0
15		**Grounds**	18370	19012.95	19678.4	20367.15	21079.998	21817.7974	22581.42	23371.77	24189.78
16				0	0	0	0	0	0	0	0.00
17		Water,Sewer		0	0	0	0	0	0	0	0.00
18		Trash		0	0	0	0	0	0	0	0.00
19		Natural Gas		0	0	0	0	0	0	0	0.00
20		Electricity		0	0	0	0	0	0	0	0.00
21		ClubH,Gates,Phone		0	0	0	0	0	0	0	0.00
22		**Utilities**	44823	46391.81	48015.52	49696.06	51435.423	53235.6633	55098.91	57027.37	59023.33
23				0	0	0	0	0	0	0	0.00
24		Insurance		0	0	0	0	0	0	0	0.00
25		Legals,banks		0	0	0	0	0	0	0	0.00
26		Tax, Fed		0	0	0	0	0	0	0	0.00
27		Tax, Property		0	0	0	0	0	0	0	0.00
28		**Legal,Ins,Tax**	3187	3298.545	3413.994	3533.484	3657.1558	3785.15626	3917.637	4054.754	4196.67
29				0	0	0	0	0	0	0	0.00
30		Repairs, Suppl, pool		0	0	0	0	0	0	0	0.00
31		Buiding mntnc		0	0	0	0	0	0	0	0.00
32		pool/ClubH		0	0	0	0	0	0	0	0.00
33		**Repairs,Supplies,**	4341	4492.935	4650.188	4812.944	4981.3973	5155.74625	5336.197	5522.964	5716.27
34				0	0	0	0	0	0	0	0.00
35		Office Supplies		0	0	0	0	0	0	0	0.00
36		Socials		0	0	0	0	0	0	0	0.00
37		**Supplies**	365	377.775	390.9971	404.682	418.8459	433.505502	448.6782	464.3819	480.64
38				0	0	0	0	0	0	0	0.00
39		**Sum Flex**	71086	73574.01	76149.10	78814.32	81572.82	84427.87	87382.84	90441.24	93606.69
40		**blncoppr inflow**	79354	102476	113020.3	106986.6	48633.751	38718.882	62276.04	74774.79	73608.107
41		**Projects**		0		0	0	0	0	0	0
42		ClubH	0	0	8000	0	0	7000	0	0	0
43		Paint ext	0	0	0	35000	35000	0	0	0	0
44		Gutters	2500	0	0	0	0	0	0	23000	0
45		Patios,sidewalks	1050	3500	3500	0	0	3500	3500	3500	3500
46		Paving E/W	10394	0	0	5000	11927	0	0		6146
47		Roofs		29446	34360	58220	0	0	0	0	0
48	added	Balconies	1800	1800	1800	0	0	0	0	0	0
49		Pool	9000	0	1000	0	0	0	5000	2500	2500
50		Tennis	0	0	0	0	0	0	10000	0	0
51		sumfix	24744	34746	49660	98220	46927	10500	18500	29000	12146
52		**GrandTotal'**	54610	67729.99	64360.89	8766.571	1706.7508	28218.882	43776.04	45774.79	61462.107
53				0	0	0	0	0	0	0	0
54		**Sum Totals**	95830	108320	124809.1	177034.3	128499.82	94927.8687	105882.8	119441.2	105752.69
55				0	0	0	0	0	0	0	0
56		BlncChecking 6/29/12		0	0	0	0	0	0	0	0
57		BlncProjects 6/29/12		0	0	0	0	0	0	0	0
58		Total Blnc		0	0	0	0	0	0	0	0
59		ForwardBlnc		0	0	0	0	0	0	0	0
60											
61		Actualdatablnc	54610	67730	64361	8767	1707	28219	43776	45775	61462

Figure 21, Capital budget for technological injections

Therefore, whatever is saved, as balance of each modular projects can be accumulated as capital project or forwarded? It will be spent on temporal capital in form of maintenances of current capital items, and technological injection capitals in new items, upgrades, and additions. In the condominium example, it could be alteration of outside electrical works into florescence lights, with a 40-60 percent saving over candlelight's electric fixture, with more light put out.

Hypothetically, the addition of heat tapes contracted for $3000 to $5000 in a cold region to divert ice and snow build up and structural damages, induces a saving of repair and replacements in coldest time of the season, which will contract for about $ 25,000. All numbers, dollars are hypotheticals example numbers, dollars, and not actuals. They are used for educational an illustrative purposes.

In modular production for automobile factory, or electronics, the technological capitals funds can go to new production possibility frontiers expansions.

Dynamic Tec-Injections Capital Budget

In the following graph, figure 22 The Tec-Inject Capital section is added. The amounts are itemized for each period, and all numbers are hypothetical numbers, and not actuals. They are used for educational purposes. The total for the tec-injections capital denoted in cell [B48] for each period is the maximum, which is spent without borrowing or deficits. Otherwise, the unit fees denoted in cells [D3to L3] will increase.

Project section denotes spending for maintenances that are accumulated funds saves per periods. Roofing [E40 to G40], $10,394, $5000, $11927 are the amounts that are spent in those periods without causing a deficit. It is true for paving, denoted in cells [D39, F&G39]. Figure 22 shows the dynamic tec-injections capital budgets.

	A	B	C	D	E	F	G	H	I	J	K	L
1		Dr. Bahman Fakhraie's © 1975-2013 , No commercial use										
2		All development and legal rights are reserved to Dr. Bahman Fakhraie										
3			unitfee	250	250	250	250	250	250	250	250	250
4			annual	132000	132000	132000	132000	132000	132000	132000	132000	132000
5	29000	bnkblnc21313		29000	59170	76640	77403.5	25716.91	22331.96	52278	71019.6	75944.67
6		Refunds,insu,fines										
7		sum inflow		161000	191170	208640	209404	157717	154332	184278	203020	207945
8		Categories		est1#s								
9		Snow			0	0	0	0	0	0	0	0
10		Lawn,snow			0	0	0	0	0	0	0	0
11		Remove,S			0	0	0	0	0	0	0	0
12		General G			0	0	0	0	0	0	0	0
13		Grounds		18370	19013	19678.4	20367.1	21080	21817.8	22581.4	23371.8	24189.78
14		Water,Sewer			0	0	0	0	0	0	0	0.00
15		Trash			0	0	0	0	0	0	0	0.00
16		Natural Gas			0	0	0	0	0	0	0	0.00
17		Electricity			0	0	0	0	0	0	0	0.00
18		ClubH,Gates,Phone			0	0	0	0	0	0	0	0.00
19		Utilities		44823	46391.8	48015.5	49696.1	51435.42	53235.66	55098.9	57027.4	59023.33
20		Insurance			0	0	0	0	0	0	0	0.00
21		Legals,banks			0	0	0	0	0	0	0	0.00
22		Tax, Fed			0	0	0	0	0	0	0	0.00
23		Tax, Property			0	0	0	0	0	0	0	0.00
24		Legal,Ins,Tax		3187	3298.55	3413.99	3533.48	3657.156	3785.156	3917.64	4054.75	4196.67
25		Repairs, Suppl, pool			0	0	0	0	0	0	0	0.00
26		Buiding mntnc			0	0	0	0	0	0	0	0.00
27		pool/ClubH			0	0	0	0	0	0	0	0.00
28		Repairs,Supplies,Po		4341	4492.94	4650.19	4812.94	4981.397	5155.746	5336.2	5522.96	5716.27
29		Office Supplies			0	0	0	0	0	0	0	0.00
30		Socials			0	0	0	0	0	0	0	0.00
31		Supplies		365	377.775	390.997	404.682	418.8459	433.5055	448.678	464.382	480.64
32		Sum Flex		71086	73574	76149	78814	81573	84428	87383	90441	93607
33		blncoppr inflow		89914	117596	132491	130589	76144.09	69904.09	96895.1	112578	114338
34		Projects			0		0	0	0	0	0	0
35		ClubH		0	0	8000	0	0	7000	0	0	0
36		Paint ext		0	0	0	35000	35000	0	0	0	0
37		Gutters		2500	0	0	0	0	0	0	23000	0
38		Patios,sidewalks		1050	3500	3500	0	0	3500	3500	3500	3500
39		Paving E/W		10394	0	0	5000	11927	0	0		6146
40		Roofs			29446	34360	58220	0	0	0	0	0
41	added	Balconies		1800	1800	1800	0	0	0	0	0	0
42		Pool		9000	0	1000	0	0	0	5000	2500	2500
43		Tennis		0	0	0	0	0	0	10000	0	0
44		sumfix		24744	34746	48660	98220	46927	10500	18500	29000	12146
45		GrandTotal*		65170	82850	83830.9	32369.2	29217.09	59404.09	78395.1	83578.3	102192
46		Sum Totals		95830	108320	124809	177034	128500	94928	105883	119441	105753
47					0	0	0	0	0	0	0	0
48	added	Tec-Inject Capital			0	0	0	0	0	0	0	0
49		New lots		2000	2070	2142.45	2217.44	2295.046	2375.373	2458.51	2544.56	2633.62
50		Elect sys		2000	2070	2142.45	2217.44	2295.046	2375.373	2458.51	2544.56	2633.62
51		NewIrrig		2000	2070	2142.45	2217.44	2295.046	2375.373	2458.51	2544.56	2633.62
52		Total /TecInjCap		6000.00	6210.00	6427.35	6652.31	6885.14	7126.12	7375.53	7633.68	7900.85
53		Actualdatablnc		59170	76640	77404	25717	22332	52278	71020	75945	94291

VerCL / VerO / VerO1 / NewV1 / Verba2 / sntv3ba / Sheet1 / BAV#3

Figure 22, Dynamic tec-injections for a capital budget

Dynamic Budgeting and Personal Finance

In chapter 1, the concept of cash flow and dynamic life cycles was introduced. The presentations of methods, formulations, applications, and budgeting have prepared the student of economic and finance for the most complicated step of the personal economy and dynamic budgeting. All numbers are hypotheticals and not actuals. They are used for educational purposes. Also, note that the numbers are constantly changing. The calculated average inflation index is set at 1.03, or 3 percent. It is used as 1.03 or its cell [G4 to O4]. Monthly and annual two income numbers are presented in the first two columns after the titles. The actual numbers can be given by the income earners for numbers and formulations. The averages for USA family income percentages, some calculated and some estimated from USA statistical book.

Figure 23 shows the teconomic of dynamic personal finance budgeting.

Clipboard | Font | Alignment

O64 | f_x | =(N63+N64)*1.03

	A	B	C	D	E	F	G	H	I	J	K	L	M	N	O
1															
2	Dr. Bahman Fakhraie's ® 1975-2013 , No commercial use								For educational examples						
3	All development and legal rights are reserved to Dr. Bahman Fakhraie								All hypothetical numbers and dollars						
4	Fiscal Year		2014		USA Family Inco		2015	2016	2017	2018	2019	2020	2021	2022	2023
5	Inflation		Monthly	Annual	Avrg %s		1.03	1.03	1.03	1.03	1.03	1.03	1.03	1.03	1.03
6	Income:				Monthl	%									
7	Wages		10000	120000			123600	127308	131127	135061.1	139112.9	143286.3	147584.9	152012.4	156572.8
8	Others		0	0											
9	Sums		10000	120000			123600	123600	123600	127308	127308	127308	131127	131127	131127
10															
11	Deductions														
12	Fed Tax		861	10332.00	$1,000	0.10	10642.0	1030.0	1030.0	10961.2	1060.9	1060.9	11290.1	1092.7	1092.7
13	State		453	5436.00	$700	0.07	5599.1	721.0	721.0	5767.1	742.6	742.6	5940.1	764.9	764.9
14	S.S.Taxes		741	8892.00	$500	0.05	9158.8	515.0	515.0	9433.5	530.5	530.5	9716.5	546.4	546.4
15	Health Ins.		100	1200	$200	0.02	1236.0	206.0	206.0	1273.1	212.2	212.2	1311.3	218.5	218.5
16	Union Fees		60	720	$150	0.00	741.6	154.5	154.5	763.8	159.1	159.1	786.8	163.9	163.9
17	Others		0	0	$300	0.03	0.0	309.0	309.0	0.0	318.3	318.3	0.0	327.8	327.8
18	Sums		2215	26580	$2,700	$0.27	27377	2936	2935.50	28199	3024	3023.57	29045	3114	3114.27
19															
20	Fixed Costs:														
21	Rnt/Mrtg/Fees		215	2580	$1,600	0.16	1200	1648	0.1648	1236	1697.44	0.169744	1273.08	1748.363	0.174836
22	Mrtg#2/Costs		800	9600	$1,100	0.11	9888	1133	0.1133	10184.64	1166.99	0.116699	10490.18	1202	0.1202
23	House Ins		19	228	$200	0.02	234.84	206	0.0206	241.8852	212.18	0.021218	249.1418	218.5454	0.021855
24	Life Ins		108	1296	$100	0.01	1334.88	103	0.0103	1374.926	106.09	0.010609	1416.174	109.2727	0.010927
25	Auto Debt		245	2940	$200	0.02	3028.2	206	0.0206	3119.046	212.18	0.021218	3212.617	218.5454	0.021855
26	Auto Ins		83	996	$200	0.02	1025.88	206	0.0206	1056.656	212.18	0.021218	1088.356	218.5454	0.021855
27	Legal/Acont		25	300	$300	0.03	309	309	0.0309	318.27	318.27	0.031827	327.8181	327.8181	0.032782
28	House Tax		59	708	$200	0.02	729.24	206	0.0206	751.1172	212.18	0.021218	773.6507	218.5454	0.021855
29	Credit Crd		0	100	$300	0.03	103	309	0.0309	106.09	318.27	0.031827	109.2727	327.8181	0.032782
30	Sums	539	1554	18648	$4,200	0.42	17853	4326	0.43	18389	4456	0.45	18940	4589	0.46
31															
32	Flex Costs:														
33	Foods		450	5400	$4,000	0.40	5562	4120	$4,120	5728.86	4243.6	4243.6	5900.726	4370.908	4370.908
34	Cloth		60	720	$100	0.01	741.6	103	$103	763.848	106.09	106.09	786.7634	109.2727	109.2727
35	Cleaners		10	120	$100	0.01	123.6	103	$103	127.308	106.09	106.09	131.1272	109.2727	109.2727
36	Hair care		77	924	$400	0.04	951.72	412	$412	980.2716	424.36	424.36	1009.68	437.0908	437.0908
37	Heat		69	828	$500	0.05	852.84	515	$515	878.4252	530.45	530.45	904.778	546.3635	546.3635
38	Elect		55	660	$500	0.05	679.8	515	$515	700.194	530.45	530.45	721.1998	546.3635	546.3635
39	Phone		192	2304	$500	0.05	2373.12	515	$515	2444.314	530.45	530.45	2517.643	546.3635	546.3635
40	Water,Swr;Etc		100	1200	$400	0.04	1236	412	$412	1273.08	424.36	424.36	1311.272	437.0908	437.0908
41	Gas/Oil		100	1200	$600	0.06	1236	618	$618	1273.08	636.54	636.54	1311.272	655.6362	655.6362
42	Car Mtnc		68	816	$500	0.05	840.48	515	$515	865.6944	530.45	530.45	891.6652	546.3635	546.3635
43	MD		125	1500	$200	0.02	1545	206	$206	1591.35	212.18	212.18	1639.091	218.5454	218.5454
44	Dentist		35	420	$100	0.01	432.6	103	$103	445.578	106.09	106.09	458.9453	109.2727	109.2727
45	Prescrip		100	1200	$200	0.02	1236	206	$206	1273.08	212.18	212.18	1311.272	218.5454	218.5454
46	School Fees		50	600	$200	0.02	618	206	$206	636.54	212.18	212.18	655.6362	218.5454	218.5454
47	Cd/Vedio/Movie:		135	1620	$100	0.01	1668.6	103	$103	1718.658	106.09	106.09	1770.218	109.2727	109.2727
48	Papers/Magz/Bk:		43	516	$100	0.01	531.48	103	$103	547.4244	106.09	106.09	563.8471	109.2727	109.2727
49	Eat Outs		40	480	$400	0.04	494.4	412	$412	509.232	424.36	424.36	524.509	437.0908	437.0908
50	Savings		100	1200	$500	0.05	1236	515	$515	1273.08	530.45	530.45	1311.272	546.3635	546.3635
51	Vacations		12	144	$100	0.01	148.32	103	$103	152.7696	106.09	106.09	157.3527	109.2727	109.2727
52	Kids Clg Fnd		100	1200	$100	0.01	1236	103	$103	1273.08	106.09	106.09	1311.272	109.2727	109.2727
53	Home Mtnc		5	60	$100	0.01	61.8	103	$103	63.654	106.09	106.09	65.56362	109.2727	109.2727
54	Family vis		12	144	$200	0.02	148.32	206	$206	152.7696	212.18	212.18	157.3527	218.5454	218.5454
55	Others		10	120	$100	0.01	123.6	103	$103	127.308	106.09	106.09	131.1272	109.2727	109.2727
56	Sums	169	1948	23376	10000		24077	10300	#####	24800	10609	10609.00	25544	10927	10927.27
57		708													
58															
59	Net		4283	51396			54292	106039	110364	55921	109220	113675	57599	112496	117085
60	Gifts/Etc		0	0			0	0	0	0	0	0	0	0	0
61	Savings		100	1200			1236	515	515	1273	530	530	1311	546	546
62	Int/Dvdnt		30	360			0	0	0	0	0	0	0	0	0
63	Sums		4413	52956			55528	106554	110879	57194	109750	114205	58910	113043	117632
64	Sums@int		1.03	52956			54544.68	113375	226527	347528	416864	542412	676316	757283	896435
65															

Figure 23, Teconomic of dynamic personal budgeting.

This personal economy presentation looks at hypotheticals for two income upper middle class family. Then an index 0f 1.03 is used for some of the cost estimation and forecasting projection.

It will give you not precise futuristic numbers, but estimation for consideration and planning strategies. In the arithmetic adjustments, whenever there are over or under estimations for items, and costs. After adjusting to the actual numbers, for example increasing the tax numbers to the actually paid numbers, the increased deference is reduces from the saving cell at (B50]. However, if there is a 50 percent decrease in the second mortgage payment in cell [B22], The 400 saved will be added the saving cell at (B50]. The same page can be used for lower single income individual. It is important to understand major purchase items will need to be delayed as saving for them will take longer. Figure 24 shows the teconomic of dynamic budgeting for single income earner.

C60 =C10-(C19+C31+C57)

	A	B	C	D	E	F	G	H	I	J	K	L	M	N	O
1															
2							THE BUGET & FORCAST ESTIMATION								
3															
4															
5	Fiscal Year		2015		USA Family Incoı		2016	2017	2018	2019	2020	2021	2022	2023	2024
6	Inflation		Monthly	Annual	Avrg %s		1.04	1.04	1.04	1.04	1.04	1.04	1.04	1.04	1.04
7	Income:				Monthly	%									
8	Wages		4132	49584			51567	53630	55775	58006	60327	62739.6	65249	67859	70573
9	Others		0	0											
10	Sums		4132	49584			51567	53630	55775	58006	60327	62739.6	65249	67859	70573
11															
12	Deductions														
13	Fed Tax		351	4214.6	$413	0.10	4383	4559	4741	4931	5128	5333	5546	5768	5999
14	State		269	3223	$289	0.07	3352	3486	3625	3770	3921	4078	4241	4411	4587
15	S.S.Taxes		310	3716.8	$207	0.05	3868	4022	4183	4350	4524	4705	4894	5089	5293
16	Health Ins.		60	720	$83	0.02	749	779	810	842	876	911	947	985	1025
17	Union Fees		40	480	$0	0.00	499	519	540	562	584	607	632	657	683
18	Others		0	0	$124	0.03	0	0	0	0	0	0	0	0	0
19	Sums		1030	12356	1,116	$0.27	12851	13365	13899	14455	15033	15635	16260	16911	17587
20															
21	Fixed Costs:														
22	Rnt/Mrtg/Fees		150	1800	$661	0.16	1872	1947	2025	2106	2190	2278	2369	2463	2562
23	Mrtg#2/Costs		700	8400	$455	0.11	8736	9085	9449	9827	10220	10629	11054	11496	11956
24	House Ins		14	168	$83	0.02	174.7	182	189	197	204	213	221	230	239
25	Life Ins		89	1068	$41	0.01	1111	1155	1201	1249	1299	1351	1405	1462	1520
26	Auto Debt		0	0	$83	0.02	0	0	0	0	0	0	0	0	0
27	Auto Ins		100	1200	$83	0.02	1248	1298	1350	1404	1460	1518	1579	1642	1708
28	Legal/Acont		10	120	$124	0.03	124.8	130	135	140	146	152	158	164	171
29	House Tax		81	972	$83	0.02	1011	1051	1093	1137	1183	1230	1279	1330	1383
30	Credit Crd		0	0	$124	0.03	0	0	0	0	0	0	0	0	0
31	Sums		$1,144	13728	1,735	0.42	14277	14848	15442	16060	16702	17370	18065	18788	19539
32															
33	Flex Costs:														
34	Foods		550	6600	1,653	0.40	6864	7139	7424	7721	8030	8351	8685	9033	9394
35	Cloth		0	0	$41	0.01	0	0	0	0	0	0	0	0	0
36	Cleaners		24	288	$41	0.01	299.5	312	324	337	350	364	379	394	410
37	Hair care		50	600	$165	0.04	624	649	675	702	730	759	790	821	854
38	Heat		61	732	$207	0.05	761.3	792	823	856	891	926	963	1002	1042
39	Elect		90	1080	$207	0.05	1123	1168	1215	1263	1314	1367	1421	1478	1537
40	Phone		139	1668	$207	0.05	1735	1804	1876	1951	2029	2111	2195	2283	2374
41	Water,Swr;Etc		0	0	$165	0.04	0	0	0	0	0	0	0	0	0
42	Gas/Oil		40	480	$248	0.06	499.2	519	540	562	584	607	632	657	683
43	Car Mtnc		40	480	$207	0.05	499.2	519	540	562	584	607	632	657	683
44	MD		40	480	$83	0.02	499.2	519	540	562	584	607	632	657	683
45	Dentist		0	0	$41	0.01	0	0	0	0	0	0	0	0	0
46	Prescrip		0	0	$83	0.02	0	0	0	0	0	0	0	0	0
47	School Fees		100	1200	$83	0.02	1248	1298	1350	1404	1460	1518	1579	1642	1708
48	Cd//Vedio/Movies		0	0	$41	0.01	0	0	0	0	0	0	0	0	0
49	Papers/Magz/Bks		15	180	$41	0.01	187.2	195	202	211	219	228	237	246	256
50	Eat Outs		91	1092	$165	0.04	1136	1181	1228	1277	1329	1382	1437	1494	1554
51	Savings		0	0	$207	0.05	0	0	0	0	0	0	0	0	0
52	Vacations		0	0	$41	0.01	0	0	0	0	0	0	0	0	0
53	Kids Clg Fnd		200	2400	$41	0.01	2496	2596	2700	2808	2920	3037	3158	3285	3416
54	Home Mtnc		0	0	$41	0.01	0	0	0	0	0	0	0	0	0
55	Family Visits		0	0	$83	0.02	0	0	0	0	0	0	0	0	0
56	Others		0	0	$41	0.01	0	0	0	0	0	0	0	0	0
57	Sums		1440	17280	N.A.	1	17971	18690	19438	20215	21024	21865	22739	23649	24595
58															
59															
60	Net		518	6219.6			6468	6727	6996	7276	7567	7870	8185	8512	8852
61	Gifts/Etc		0	0			0	0	0	0	0	0	0	0	0
62	Savings		0	0			0	0	0	0	0	0	0	0	0
63	Int/Dvdnt		30	360			374.4	389	405	421	438	456	474	493	512
64	Sums		548.3	6579.6			6843	7116	7401	7697	8005	8325	8658	9005	9365
65	Sums@int		1.03	6579.6			6777	14028	21850	30203	39114	48613	58730	69496	80946

Figure 24, Teconomic of dynamic budgets for one income.

The main difference will be items that cannot be saved for or afforded by lower income earners, and reduced saving by the lower single income earners. Nevertheless, in year 2020, cell [K66], Up to $ 39,000 is spendable. That is five-year saving, if all the numbers, costs, and revenues change per assumption. The purchase of a new car will change auto expenses and taxes, and other assumptive numbers have to alter in the planning.

In 9 years after 2015 the hypothetical initial year of planning, if no major costs accrue outside the assumptive boundaries, by year 2024 the individual can spend $ 80,000 on a one-time technological injection purchase.

In figure 25, the blank spreadsheet is presented, with formulation added. It is ready for the first column numbers to be added. It will forecast for 3 percent inflation adjustment of the numbers.

Figure 25 shows a null spreadsheet for teconomic of null teconomic of dynamic of personal budget.

C57 =SUM(C34:C56)

	A	B	C	D	E	F	G	H	I	J	K	L	M	N	O
1															
2							THE BUGET & FORCAST ESTIMATION								
3															
4															
5	Fiscal Year		2010		USA Family Incom		2021	2022	2023	2024	2025	2026	2027	2028	2029
6	Inflation		Monthly	Annual	Avrg %s		1.04	1.04	1.04	1.04	1.04	1.04	1.04	1.04	1.04
7	Income:				Monthly	%									
8	Wages		0	0			0	0	0	0	0	0	0	0	0
9	Others		0	0											
10	Sums		0	0			0	0	0	0	0	0	0	0	0
11															
12	Deductions														
13	Fed Tax		0	0	$0	0.10	0	0	0	0	0	0	0	0	0
14	State		0	0	$0	0.07	0	0	0	0	0	0	0	0	0
15	S.S.Taxes		0	0	$0	0.05	0	0	0	0	0	0	0	0	0
16	Health Ins.		0	0	$0	0.02	0	0	0	0	0	0	0	0	0
17	Union Fees		0	0	$0	0.00	0	0	0	0	0	0	0	0	0
18	Others		0	0	$0	0.03	0	0	0	0	0	0	0	0	0
19	Sums		0	0	$0	$0.27	0	0	0	0	0	0	0	0	0
20															
21	Fixed Costs:														
22	Rnt/Mrtg/Fees		0	0	$0	0.16	0	0	0	0	0	0	0	0	0
23	Mrtg#2/Costs		0	0	$0	0.11	0	0	0	0	0	0	0	0	0
24	House Ins		0	0	$0	0.02	0	0	0	0	0	0	0	0	0
25	Life Ins		0	0	$0	0.01	0	0	0	0	0	0	0	0	0
26	Auto Debt		0	0	$0	0.02	0	0	0	0	0	0	0	0	0
27	Auto Ins		0	0	$0	0.02	0	0	0	0	0	0	0	0	0
28	Legal/Accnt		0	0	$0	0.03	0	0	0	0	0	0	0	0	0
29	House Tax		0	0	$0	0.02	0	0	0	0	0	0	0	0	0
30	Credit Crd		0	0	$0	0.03	0	0	0	0	0	0	0	0	0
31	Sums		0	0	$0	0.42	0	0	0	0	0	0	0	0	0
32															
33	Flex Costs:														
34	Foods		0	0	$0	0.40	0	0	0	0	0	0	0	0	0
35	Cloth		0	0	$0	0.01	0	0	0	0	0	0	0	0	0
36	Cleaners		0	0	$0	0.01	0	0	0	0	0	0	0	0	0
37	Hair care		0	0	$0	0.04	0	0	0	0	0	0	0	0	0
38	Heat		0	0	$0	0.05	0	0	0	0	0	0	0	0	0
39	Elect		0	0	$0	0.05	0	0	0	0	0	0	0	0	0
40	Phone		0	0	$0	0.05	0	0	0	0	0	0	0	0	0
41	Water,Swr,Etc		0	0	$0	0.04	0	0	0	0	0	0	0	0	0
42	Gas/Oil		0	0	$0	0.06	0	0	0	0	0	0	0	0	0
43	Car Mtnc		0	0	$0	0.05	0	0	0	0	0	0	0	0	0
44	MD		0	0	$0	0.02	0	0	0	0	0	0	0	0	0
45	Dentist		0	0	$0	0.01	0	0	0	0	0	0	0	0	0
46	Prescrip		0	0	$0	0.02	0	0	0	0	0	0	0	0	0
47	School Fees		0	0	$0	0.02	0	0	0	0	0	0	0	0	0
48	Cd/Vedio/Movies		0	0	$0	0.01	0	0	0	0	0	0	0	0	0
49	Papers/Magz/Bks		0	0	$0	0.01	0	0	0	0	0	0	0	0	0
50	Eat Outs		0	0	$0	0.04	0	0	0	0	0	0	0	0	0
51	Savings		0	0	$0	0.05	0	0	0	0	0	0	0	0	0
52	Vacations		0	0	$0	0.01	0	0	0	0	0	0	0	0	0
53	Kids Clg Fnd		0	0	$0	0.01	0	0	0	0	0	0	0	0	0
54	Home Mtnc		0	0	$0	0.01	0	0	0	0	0	0	0	0	0
55	Family Visits		0	0	$0	0.02	0	0	0	0	0	0	0	0	0
56	Others		0	0	$0	0.01	0	0	0	0	0	0	0	0	0
57	Sums		0	0		1	0	0	0	0	0	0	0	0	0
58															
59															
60	Net		0	0			0	0	0	0	0	0	0	0	0
61	Gifts/Etc		0	0			0	0	0	0	0	0	0	0	0
62	Savings		0	0			0	0	0	0	0	0	0	0	0
63	Int/Dvdnt		0	0			0	0	0	0	0	0	0	0	0
64	Sums		0	0			0	0	0	0	0	0	0	0	0
65	Sums@int		1.03	0			0	0	0	0	0	0	0	0	0

Figure 25, A blank teconomic of dynamic personal budget.

All readers begin all good personal economic planning, with blank screen, a blank page, in order to remind the readers, all hard works are starting here, after you acquire the knowledge. That is (always) the beginning of hard work. Cell [C57] shows zero, but the formulation (=sum (C34:C56) in the active window in figure 25 shows it, and as we add the real numbers the formula will add them up. The important second shoe is applying it diligently to your personal finances, and the required record keeping that dove tails in your successful financial lives.

Students of finance, banking, and economic and experienced business people, small and large business owners already know the importance of budgeting in all dynamic life cycle events, and all modular productions. The readers of this book should internalize the importance of these practices to improve their own economic lives.

Notes

[1] Bahman Fakhraie, PhD., TECONOMICS,
ISBN/EAN13: 0985295813 / 9780985295813,
https://www.createspace.com/4196760
Dr. Bahman Fakhraie, Technological injection, dynamic new capital measurements, and Production Theory in Economics, (Michigan: ProQuest LLC, 2010) and, 94,
https://order.proquest.com/OA_HTML/pqdtibeCCtpItmDspRte.jsp
Dr. Bahman Fakhraie's books web page link,
http://bahfecon.wix.com/bahfecon

[2] John A. Hopkin, Ph.D., Peter j. Barry, Ph.D., C.B. Baker, Ph.D., Finical Management In Agriculture,(Danville, Illinois: the Interstates Printers & Publishers, Inc.,131-135

[3] Authors books can illuminate the subject in more details, Bahman Fakhraie, PhD., *DEMAND AND SUPPLY SIDES OF TECHNOLOGICAL INJECTIONS,* ISBN-978-0-9852958-3-7,
http://www.amazon.com/Demand-supply-Sides-Technological-Injections/dp/098529583X/ref=sr_1_4?ie=UTF8&qid=1360206619&sr=8-4&keywords=BAHMAN+FAKHRAIE
Bahman Fakhraie, PhD., *TECONOMICS,*
ISBN/EAN13: 0985295813 / 9780985295813,
https://www.createspace.com/4196760
Dr. Bahman Fakhraie's books web page link,
http://bahfecon.wix.com/bahfecon

[4] Circular-flow, velocity of money, RDI, real growth attest.

[5] Author formulated these worksheet exercises.

CHPTER 7

Innovational Elements of Financial Management

The importance of economic budgeting is the next step after producing something for barter or exchange. The complicities of modern lives and possibilities for modular productions contribute to such a need for complex record keeping and budgeting.

The expansive additions via innovational means and technological injections to productions, in addition to contributive effects of arts and sciences to production make economic budgeting indispensable.

Property for exchange

These complicated human endeavors of economic exchanges are constituted on simple concept of trade, barter, and exchange of goods and services of value, transaction of personal property, goods, and services for things of value like notes or money.

The metamorphosis of barter or agreements into legal contracts, which is upheld by law, is interwoven in human history of misbehaving and behavioral history. From war booties and cave-to-cave or village to village tribal war raids, to modern day frauds, internet or ID frauds humanity has learned to establish legal definitions. Nobility, creed, ethic, and even theological morality vanish faster than flees without the sunlight of transparency, media focus, or twitting and multimedia coverage. It is not a surprise that cultures, societies, civilizations, which have crawled further from the ethical foundation, find their progress vacuous and fleeting.

Since, the bazar markets of Persia, and international caravan trades of Persia, Arabia and Asia, and the water trades from the East to West and Northwest and back, there have been verbal promissory and then written notes and instruments of finance. Human history has built on solid needed-honesty, trusts, clear definitions, and the promissory notes, contracts, and legal agreements have resolved conflicts, and have assisted exchanges of property, goods, and services, and repetition of commerce in human history. Those have been foundational for economic success, economic growth, and development of industrious societies.

Personal property is defined under, tangibles and intangibles property, they both can be used as collateral for loans.

Tangible are defines as,

- Products held for individual consumption,
- Households' consumptions items,
- Equipment capital items,
- Inventory input items held,
- All items held for lease, sale, or contracts,
- All farm products

- Homemade products jam jars, etc.
- Woodwork art, art works, writing, etc.

Intangibles are defines as,

a) Contract rights, notes and papers,
b) Accounts receivable, negotiated papers,
c) Instruments of value with notes,
d) Patent and copyright certificates,
e) Esoteric, rare or remote value items

Contracts

The agreements for transaction require certain characteristic validities, before they are considered legal contracts. That is they are legally enforceable.

Different localities, states, providence, or countries may differ in legal definition of contracts. They usual need to adhere to certain elements.[1] The main reason for that are those principalities, and then they have to enforce the contracts in case of conflict, nonpayment, and refusal to respect those contracts by either parties, or entities signatory to the same contracts.

The important parts of legal contracts, which make them legally enforceable by local courts or municipalities, are as follows,

- Both parties are of legal age,
- Parties are competent,
- They are Identifiable
- They meet Residency
- Legal guarantors, or guardians,
- Trustees,
- There must be a clear offer
- There must be acceptance of the same offer,
- And a counter offer of value in exchange,
- Both offer and counter offer must legal,
- Consideration or counter offer is sufficient.

The value of the contracts must be over certain amount, and the duration of exchanges must be over a year, which these will determine the need that it be in written form to be valid, or legally enforceable.

Summary and Some Conclusions

President John F. Kennedy stated, "Problems are people made and people can fix them." It is true now, that people can make their problems much bigger by technological injections. Nevertheless, the technological injections can also assist to undo a lot of the big harm, as well. If we allow scientific evaluations and established assumptive truth guideposts to guide the people, greed will not countermand or replace the facts lightly. There is a need for further detail studies of embryonic non-carbon energy resources, and transformation stages and plans of action. The size of such a project and its colossal significances as a technological leap scribes it as a government funded initial mega-project. However, it will be a mistake to assume, their numerous potential profitable and commercial offshoots can be contained. The positive externalities associated with such technological injections will permeate and benefit the free markets globally.

Private and Governmental Constructional-ism

Once again the economic science discoveries guides towards post-Schumpeterian macroeconomic private and governmental reparative constructional-ism.

Another wartime president Dwight D. Eisenhower's war experience alerted us to another pitfall of history. Nations can waste time and efforts on political and deficit polemics, while wasting trillions harming other human beings around the globe, and still end up in the darkness of one kind or another, and economically broke, and still without prioritized viable solutions.

After all, they still need to spend fortunes and help others to rebuilt back to the same place of history, where they lost their sanity in the first place, or where nature took them.

The interstate highways infrastructure-projects part of government-private infrastructure-plans of President Dwight D. Eisenhower, a republican war hero propelled USA economy into present millennium. American voters should show little patience for those whom wear down his political party label with small-minded narrowness of visions and plans, and miserliness in their anti-science views of American futuristic national purpose. Humanity is in a global competitive scientific and technologically alerted state of advancement. Those self-imposed devolutionary retrogressions will prove the most costly.

Governments as almost all manufactured tools, systems, and services have appropriate functionalities. There are skills, educations, retraining, job creations, and upgrades associated with all technological injections, which will modify their negative externalities.

The dynamic budgeting at the individual helps the individuals' economy for a limited time. It cannot replace the macroeconomics consequences of governmental misadventures, or major structural devolutionary alteration to employment for long.

There are luddites whom are displaced by new technologies, or displace the new modular production processes with structural changes for the economy. That is why governmental tax and transfers were designed to assists even advanced economies by retraining and job-placements.

It is the height of irony, if they are the same group, which scream the most about governmental expansionism. Because they are the ones needing the transitory government retraining, unemployment, educational aids, foods stamps, and health care assistance the most, until they can land new jobs.

The higher income earners, the main benefiters of modern technological injections, are also luddites, if they refuse to pay their minimal shares in taxes, which will fortify the circular flow and increase the velocity of money in the economy. Thus ensures the necessary, sufficient, and sustainability conditions of production in a viable and growing economy in the more perfect times.

The importance of government in such an economy cannot be minimized or constantly be undermined, without structural harmful consequences. The industrial economies placement in human history is not due to probability chances, denomination, theological miracles, or even ethical exceptionalism. It is by accumulated human knowledge and the result of many failed social, political, and economic experimentations, and more than thousands of lives. It can also all be fleeting in ignorance.

From Persian empires establishment, from Japanese and Chinese tribal warlords, to Mongolians' invasions, to Chinese Maoism, French revolution and pre and post Stalin communist experimentalism, American Indian colonialism, to slavery and religious wars, to Europeans Afro-Asiatic colonialism, to world war one and two, a lot of history has accumulated, and a lot of human knowledge has been advanced. Accumulations of human knowledge have had extraordinary expensive price tag in cadavers and lives, treasures, and livelihoods during these epochs.

The triumph of scientific discoveries and advancement of philosophical curiosity without being burned for them are fairly known, but new in these voluminous epochs of barbarisms mentioned. That is the void of accumulated human knowledge have had an expensive collateral costs.[2] Despite inclinations of ideological simpletons and science deniers, societies ought to respect the true value of science and scientists, social scientists, and educators, because they will be the ultimate victims of their lack of academic, scientific, and intellectual curiosities.

Since the age of enlightenment to present, advancements against diseases, famine, genocidal idiocies have occurred. The knowledge has also advanced the technological skill for massive self-destructions at an increasing tempo in a shortened time span.

Therefore, the vigilance against ignorance-biases of humanity, and the tenacity toward self-destruction have not been irradiated, but they have been tampered mildly. The responsibilities are left at conscious educated minds to stay intellectually free, politically alert, and well informed to navigate the choppy seas of ignorance and the storms of ill winds. Technological injection can help advance the good lives for many, but it can also be used to taken advantage of many. Therefore, the constant need for everlasting vigilance is the oxygen of democracy. Figure 26 shows the influences of technological injections in a fully functional modern economy. Figure 27 shows dynamic circular flow of incomes and revenues in the fully functional modern economy, and the importance of governmental economic presence in modern time.

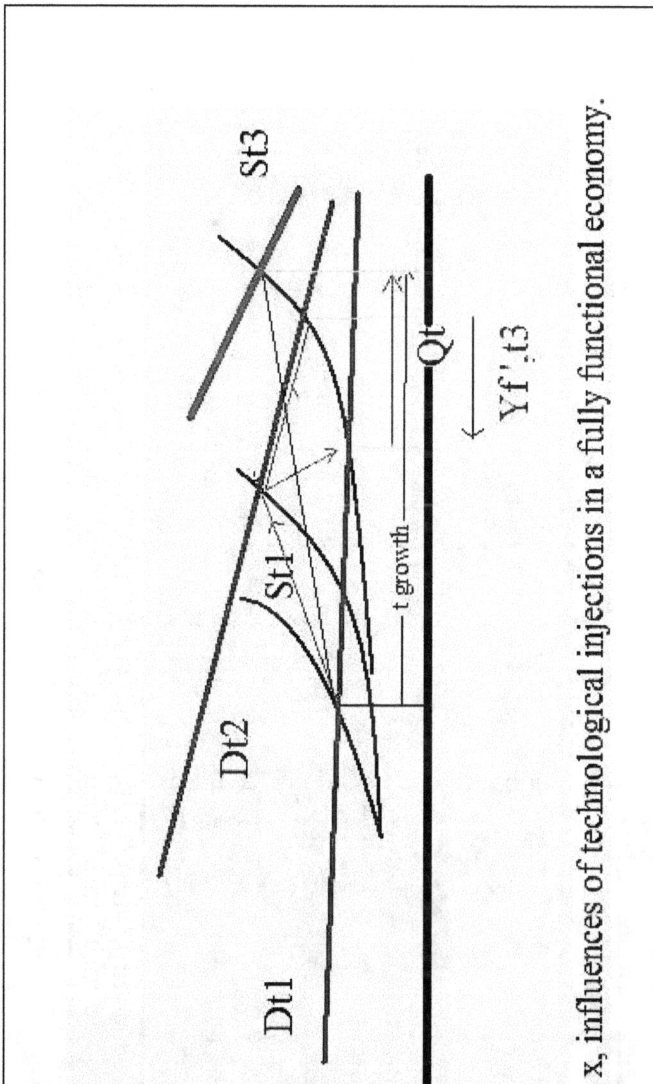

Figure 26, Technological injections, and economy.

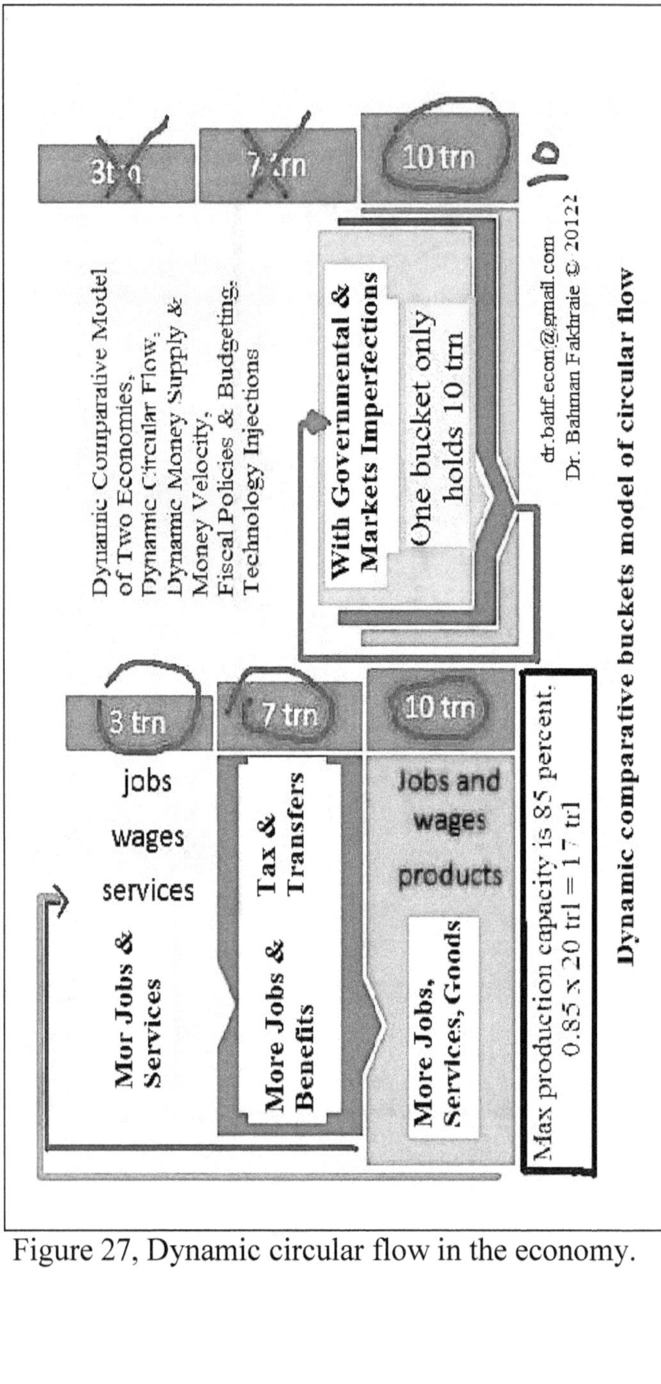

Figure 27, Dynamic circular flow in the economy.

The rest of population can agree with them about the intrusions, the taxation without representations, militarizing of domestic economies, legislative process, judiciary, commerce, and all other overt and documented malfeasances. Nevertheless, on retraining and job creations, investment in infrastructure, health, and public safety issues, investment in research and scientific discoveries, and on educational opportunities, they are mistaken.

Certain less trained economists include national defense readily and unguardedly, when it is appropriate and well balanced. Since history obliges, it obviously tend to dominate and parasitically destroy the hosts economies, and replace evolutionarily invented and perfected democratic checks and balances, with controls and commands system, which define dictatorships and cultivate non-democratic governmental organizations. Those are many steps away from the market perfect competition demand and supply dependency-signal systems. Thus, they are increasingly inefficient imperfect competitions and monopolistic none-free markets.

People do understand very well, that nature will humble humanity at every bad turn, that is why humanity comes together and combines their energy, resources, and funds (tax and transfers by governments, decent livable salaries by private businesses) to rebuild, reinvest in innovative means of productions.[3] This is called exchange theory, or redistributive value theory under economics subjects, yet it makes distinction between constructive wealth creation and exchange theory of value (jobs and living wages), and nonproductive wealth concentrations (Criminal enterprises, governmental, organizational monopolistic power-systems and organizations), which will transfer (redistribute) wealth often upwards to a limited selected (elite, wealthy, politico or military) classes. Even in the modern none Marxists unorthodox economic theories this is occurring, as a complement to orthodox economics, including the classics.

Dynamic Budgeting and Innovation Process

It is important to realize human economic history evolved from holding gold and it immobility, to using notes (a promissory note) about the amount of gold holdings, to notes as paper money, for the influence of increased velocity of money in expansion of commerce. Both the Republicans (Presidents Lincoln civil war greenback notes, Nixon abolishing gold standards) and democratic presidents (FDR) upheld these progressions out of the necessity of the epochal historical times.

People depend on scientific discovery of nature, and allow for governmental combination of reasonable resources and revenues to countermand natural disasters, and people made economic and financials' cyclical catastrophes and calamities. In this study, an innovative model is presented to devise methodologies to countermand these cyclical calamities, with some degree of success.

The federal, state, and local governments are all of us, so are the insurance cooperation under private contracts that pay for some rebuilding, warehouses, grocery stores, supplies of goods and services are linked to us by the economy as well.

Unfortunately, due to naiveties and ideological fervor, elemental aspects of government organizations take these periodic dependencies and new technological capabilities for intrusive internal power-grabs, and uncontrolled expansionism. When these or other forms of militarism turn inward, they often prove too dangerous to the stability of democratic entities and too expensive on the economic systems.

All the businesses require the government services to reestablish their market links and supply routes, and infrastructures, before they can get there close to all of us.

This is also true, when market demands cascades down ward, as they did in 1930s USA-depression experiences and more so recently.

Nevertheless, it will take the governments some time to get there, under national and natural emergency conditions.[4] A set of modular production processes starting at thought-action level, and fulfilling all three lemma, including sustainability lemma.[5] Dr. Bahman Fakhraie presented those conditions, in the studies that advanced the new lemma of sustainability.[6] This was as an addition to Sheppard lemmas necessary and sufficiency conditions for new economic orthodoxy of production optimizations. The economic inner core, which are explain in Dr. Bahman Fakhraie mathematical model meeting Necessary, Sufficient, Maximization, Optimization, and Sustainable lemma.

Dr. Bahman Fakhraie reintroduces them in this newer model. They add to the organizational, finance, and marketing complex-infrastructures, which evolved around product development from ideas to inventions to marketable products.

Therefore, in figure 22 and figure 28, show the innovational links between dynamic budgeting, temporal investments, and innovational synthesis and synchronizations complex relationships in modular production processes. There are substantial alterations that will take place in transformative two stage innovational alteration, which will have to take shape as technological injections transform the macro-production possibility frontiers' topography. Most new students of economics will miss the cognitive interrelationships. However, when they make the intellectual journey a few times, they will appreciate the discoveries.

Figure 28 shows Dr. Bahman Fakhraie economic model of conversions of idea to inventions and marketable products.

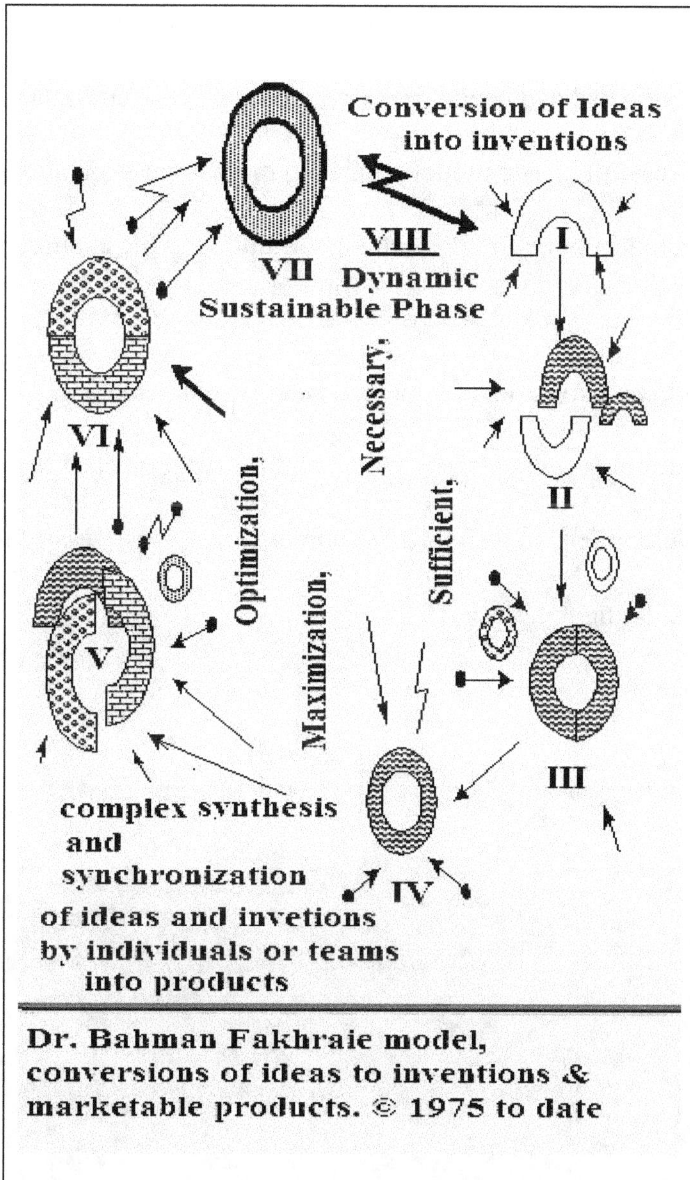

Figure 28, economic model of conversions of idea to inventions and marketable products.

It is vitally important to basic comprehension that the models have been applied to modular production theory successfully. The model applies to most innovational modular production projects. In additions to the examples in this book, it has been useful in original book writings, published book development, academic mathematical modeling, movie script writing, and movie project development, as well as development and growth theory in developing nations.

Notes

[1] Hopkin, J. A., Barry, P. J., and Baker, C. B., Financial Management in Agriculture, Interstate Printers & Publisher, Inc. 1973, pp. 21-27

[2] Dr. Bahman Fakhraie, Teconomics: the microeconomic analysis, Utah, FERDAT publishing 2012, and, https://www.createspace.com/4196760, Books web page at, http://bahfecon.wix.com/bahfecon

[3] Dr. Bahman Fakhraie, *Analytical Remedies for The Millennial Cascading Economic Declines,* Utah FERDAT Publishing 2012, and at,
https://www.createspace.com/4187823,
Books web page at, http://bahfecon.wix.com/bahfecon#

[4] Dr. Bahman Fakhraie, *Teconomics: the microeconomic analysis*, Utah, FERDAT publishing 2012, and, https://www.createspace.com/4196760, Books web page at, http://bahfecon.wix.com/bahfecon

[5] Dr. Bahman Fakhraie, *Technological injection, dynamic new capital measurements, and Production Theory in Economics*, (Michigan: ProQuest LLC, 2010) and, https://order.proquest.com/OA_HTML/pqdtibeCCtpItmDspRte.jsp
Dr. Bahman Fakhraie's books web page is at, http://bahfecon.wix.com/bahfecon

[6] Appendix of this work continues the mathematical presentations.
Teconomics of Verbalism, Utah FERDAT Publishing 2012, and at, https://www.createspace.com/4121720,
Books web page at, http://bahfecon.wix.com/bahfecon

Appendix

A

ARITHMATIC OF OPTIMIZATION

The series of mathematical analysis are presented henceforth, to study utility optimization and demand side, and production optimization and the supply side analysis. The traditional mathematical evaluation for optimization analysis is as follows:

Traditional productions function,

$$o = f(v_i^{\varepsilon})$$

Necessary condition, it is also known as the first order condition (FOC):

$$f'(v_i^{\varepsilon}) > 0$$

Sufficient condition, it is also known as secondary condition (SOC):

$$f''(v_i^{\varepsilon}) > 0$$

The traditional production function is with mathematical evaluation for optimization analysis.

Conditions in Case of Growth

$$o = f(v_i^{\varepsilon})$$

Necessary condition:

$$f'(v_i^{\varepsilon}) > 0$$

Sufficient condition:

$$f''(v_i^{\varepsilon}) > 0$$

Implication: the function is positive and increasing at the increasing rate.

Condition in Case of Decay

$$o = f(v_i^{\varepsilon})$$

Necessary condition:

$$f'(v_i^{\varepsilon}) > 0$$

Sufficient condition:

$$f''(v_i^{\varepsilon}) < 0$$

Implication: the function is positive and increasing at the decreasing rate.

B

ARITHMATIC OF TIME

Lagrange analysis of n-variables and multi-constraints Lagrange multipliers the following is the mathematical analysis of productive use of available entrepreneurial times, on daily bases. Individuals have to make decision in time-use management, between productive choices they have to make in use of the fixed 24 hours.

They make assumptive choices about their time uses, for required sleep, and time lot spent on education, and required work for income, as the following relations show. However, in post emergency or post disaster time, other arrangements have to be made to replace the collateral losses, and the income earning time. Churches Mosques, Temples, and governmental and none governmental (NGOs) have had a historical rule.

$$f(X_S X_E X_W) = Q_i$$

$$g(X_S X_E X_W) = 24$$

$$h(X_S X_E X_W) = y_0$$

$$Z = f(X_S X_E X_W) + \mu[(24 - g(X_S X_E X_W)] + \gamma[(y_0 - h(X_S X_E X_W)] = 0$$

$$Qi = f(Xi)$$

$$g(Xi) = 24$$

$$h(Xi) = y_0$$

$$Z\mu = 24 - g(Xi) = 0$$

$$Z\gamma = y_0 - h(Xi) = 0$$

$$Zi = fi - \mu\, gi - \gamma\, hi = 0$$

Arithmetical Proof:

FOC

$$\vartheta Z^1 = 0$$

SOC

$$\vartheta Z^2 < 0$$

All constants are great than zero.

C

MAXIMIZATION OF GAINS, OPTIMIZATION OF VALUE

Budget determines expenditure on costs of production of X, and Y. Y can be designated governmental, or NGO injection in new innovational capital, while X, is some local productions still operational, which must be encouraged to keep the level of economic activities high to accommodate the post technological-injection economy. λ1 is unit costs.

$$B = \lambda1\ X1 + \lambda2Y2$$

S denotes level of skills, technological injections required. In this example, λ2 denotes the skill level of NGOs, or governmental units presented at the scene of disasters. In some nations, local skill or technologies are not able to present the type of presence, which the post disaster conditions demand. Geographically isolated areas require naval assets, which are not present in most countries to meet the logistic demands of post disaster conditions.

S = s1 X2 + s2 Y2

Education and retraining required in use capital productively.

$$E_k = e1\ k_X + e2\ k_Y$$

Production function is,

$$Q = f(X, Y : \dot{B}, \dot{S}, \dot{E})$$

The Lagrange equation is,

$$Z_Q = f(Vi) + \mu i\ [(\dot{B} - \lambda i\ Vi)] + \mu j\ [(\dot{S} - \lambda j\ Vj)] + \mu l\ [(\dot{E}_k - \lambda l\ Vl)]$$

FOC

$$d\,Z_Q/dt = 0$$

SOC

$$d^2 Z_Q\ /\ d^2 t < 0$$

More assumptive conditions are as follows,

All constants > 0

OPTIMIZATION OF VALUE

Optimization of Value Ψ is a function of maximization of profit, minimization of costs, and optimization of social welfare function of Vi.

$$\Psi = f(\max \pi, \min C, \text{opt } Ui)$$

$$Ui = f(qxi, qyi : Cvi : Bi, -/+?)$$

And

$$Ui = f(+, 0, -/+?)$$

COMPENSATORY SUSTAINABILITY CONDITIONS

Individual Utility Function

$$Ui = f(+, 0, -/+?)$$

The utility of individual Vi is improved in consumption of Qxi, while the consumption of Qyi stays the same, and the budget line can improve, stay the same, or become negative, thus also influencing the utility function.

Social Welfare Function of Group Utilities

$$\text{Opt } SWFvi, SWFvi = f(Ui, Uj, Ul, -/+?)$$

Majority of group utility will be better off at a new position A, therefore, they will agree to the project. The utility of some of group utility will stay the same. They stay either satisfy or join the last groups at position B. The utility of some of group will be worst off, there has to be tradeoffs, as in exchanges, higher remunerations, or tax-transfer strategies to optimize the experiences of all involved for them to agree to move to the better position A. This is another clause added to the arguments for sustainability conditions in all economic system orthodox or unorthodox, holistically.

SUSTAINABILITY CONDITIONS of TECHNOLOGICAL INJECTIONS

Let us take a little time to study some of the sustainability conditions of investment in innovational new capital, with respect to social welfare functions for the group utility functions, for all individual in the group. Two positions are A, and B, such that A is better than B.

$$A > B$$

Therefore, A is preferred to B,

$$\therefore A\ P\ B$$

$$SWFvi = f\,(Ui, Uj, Ul, -/+?)$$

The benefits sustainability conditions are as follows,

1. Sustainably condition universal criteria, it is if at least one individual utility function improves at A, others feel no change, then → A, A > B.
2. Sustainably condition Kaldorian criteria, this is when those in position A, pay, bribe, exchange with losers for the move to A, since A P B, then A > B. Alternatively, they offer to aid at their time of need.
3. Sustainably condition Hicks criteria, those losing from move to A, cannot bribe the groups to keep them from moving to A, therefore APB, → A, A > B.

4. Sustainably condition Scitovsky criteria, if the gainers can compensate (promise to help later) some of the losers. Moreover, some of the losers cannot bribe any of the winners from the move to A. The move will take place. Such that A P B, hence, →A, A>B.
5. Sustainably condition Dr. Bahman Fakhraie criteria, or the dynamic sustainably universal criteria, (NGOs or Gs assist production to operational levels) that technological injection will improve all utilities positions proportionally, such that [∀ Ui at A] P B, then →A, A>B. For some future post-functionality arrangements, (as tax and transfers).

There are more studies under welfare economic theory, and potential economic dissertational works.

D

RATES OF GROWTH AND DECAY

r* = (Xt2-Xt1)/Xt1

$$r = \frac{\ln Xt2 - \ln Xt1}{lnXt1}$$

$$Ey, ms = \frac{\frac{\delta y}{\delta t}}{\frac{\delta ms}{\delta t}}$$

FERDAT, AND LEGALS

FAKHRAIE EDUCATION RESEARCH
DEVELOPMENT AND TRUST

FERDT

FERDAT

Fakhraie Education Research
Development And Trust

Organization, Fakhraie Bahman

Grant proposal by

Bahman Fakhraie, PhD, ©, ®, ™

Budgetary, Managerial Directive and Legal Clauses

Legal letter and charges for unauthorized information use.

Section 1, Mission Statement

Section 2, Budgetary Clause

Section 3, Managerial Clause

Section 4, Legal Clause

Section 5, Organization Chart

Section 6, Data Management

Section 7, Vita

Legal letter is in cases of e-fraud, misuse of firms' information, or harm under sec. G. All linked and relaying entities, institutions, governmental agencies are accountable no exception.

Dear Sirs, persons, INC., (illegal use of firms' info), your current bill is **$10,000, ≤Ceiling $60 mils.** On behalf of Dr. Bahman Fakhraie, FERDAT, and the firm, family trusts.

These are the current charges related to illegal e-fraud and all harmful misuse of firms information, after the first time we asked you to terminate all contract and remove our name, firms' name etc. on this date.

1-Illegal use, the unapproved initial use of firm's name, contact name, duns #, any and all information supplied to USA government for the sole purpose of firm doing business with USA government, grant.gov, and NSF, Universities, other governmental and tribal entities, and all grantors. Minimum charges are $10,000.00, up to the ceiling of $ 60 million.

2-Use of firm contacts, names, address phone #, TIN/#s, and any information related to that.

Minimum charges are $10,000.00, up to the ceiling of $60 mils.

3- Continuation after repeated formal request to terminate illegal actions, sending junk e-mail, junk mail, forcing this firm to send back, by mail and certified mail. Legal costs related to that.

Minimum charges are $10,000.00 per each event, up to the ceiling of $60 mils.

4- Interference with firm soul business, time sensitive writing of government and private grants, at grant.gov, and NSF, universities, private foundations, NGOs and all grantors, with 4.5 million dollars floor. The Minimum charges are 4.5 million dollars, up to the ceiling of $60 mils.

4- Absolute or required non-disclosures by the firm or Dr. Fakhraie will require pre-paid plan with minimum flooring pay. Flex-legalism targeted at the firm, or Dr. B. Fakhraie will be due cause for nonpaid termination by the same, and harm-terms of Sec G of private contracts.
6- Punitive damages are up to 60 million dollars, if you do not stop, after the first notification.
Please make an effort to pay your bill. There will be additional charges added and sent to you for each time you try to contact the same entities, after the same dated termination notices.
Dr. BF, this is part of the legal notices under sec G, or formal termination notice dates.

Section 1, Mission Statement
To formulate optimum functionality in management teams, in order to make profitable and beneficial contributions, and create opportunity for merited advancements, **to advance research** in my fields of study. Utilizing rare combination of theory and empiricism, cultivated in multi-cultural inclusive settings in academic and private enterprises, I enhance the management in productivity and completion of productive projects, or suggest corrective recursive evaluation and total quality control improvements.
Experiences, among fields of International Trade, Managerial, and Production theories in Economics, Finance, Personal Finance management, and Businesses, which modern business and academic institutions find very expensive to employ and too costly not to employ. My extensive backgrounds help me advance research in my fields of study.
Section 2, Budgetary Clause

* All initial dedicated deposits (inflows) will be transferred to a FREDT, or FREDAT business account.

* No allotments or contracts activity will take place, until full transfer of funds has taken place per contracts. The cash-accounting method is used for tax purposes.
* Alteration to submit to requirements and regulations will fully transfer all risks, fees, and penalties, and legal responsibilities, to the source of the requirements.

* There will be a minimum product list, or writing, or proposal-output for further research, which will be presented and agreed to at the initial phases.
* This will be the only output legally required at the end of contract, or at the end of grant periods.
* There is a managerial flow chart enclosed to enhance comprehensions of cash flow, read after the legal notes section.

Section 3, Managerial Clause

* Dr. Bahman Fakhraie will act as agent, manger, and soul administrator, Executives director, Principle Investigator PI for FERDT, FERDAT, Fakhraie Bahman Organization, with full rights to take legal action and make final settlement on its accounts.
* Dr. Bahman Fakhraie will act as agent, manger, and soul administrator for Fakhraie Bahman Organization, with full right to take legal action on its accounts.
* A general electronic bookkeeping is followed, on periodical bases, as grants require it. Current standard is quarterly, post full disbursements of grant funding. (FRR is required quarterly)
* Details, information, managerial technologies are legally protected, and no such disclosure will be made of the Organization, administrator, assignees, or representatives of FERDT, FERDAT, or Fakhraie Bahman Organization. All copyright materials are

marketable, or further developed by Mr. Fakhraie. All existing rights are reserved.

* All informal and formal requests can be made by mail, or email.
* There is forfeiture of all advances, in cases of mortality, health, or attempt at disbarment, legal action, harm, against soul administrator, Fakhraie Bahman Organization, with full right to take legal action on its accounts.
* Any and all such request will have to forward additional funding for legal representations and undue imposition of costs or harm, please read the legal note and sec. G. It will always apply.
* Alteration to submit to requirements and regulations will fully transfer all risks, fees, and penalties, and legal responsibilities, to the source of the requirements.

* The reviewers will have access to a portion of the progress.
* Full transparencies are practiced for authorized agents only, mostly through the internet, after proper signatures are obtained.
* All future development, educational development will have to be contracted, or signed out temporarily.
* All copyrights and proprietary rights are reserved, granted, accorded to Dr. Bahman Fakhraie, and his living trust.
* The final product in initial agreement will be shared with the grantors, after all the financial settlements have been met.

* PI, FERDAT; Dr. Fakhraie, Bahman
Dr. Bahman Fakhraie, PhD, UOU, UT, USA
* Position Classification, Executive level I,
* Salary exceeds Fed Cap for private contracts.
* NSF ID, 000586796, Organizational ID Code, P 269878425
* Private for Profit Business:
* DUNS Number D&B # ████89684,
* CAGE/NCAGE: ███S3, Congressional Districts, UT_001
* Sec G of private contract always applies
* For other institutional DUNS, etc. Please, check cover letter, or contact PI. Thanks
* PI Information(dated)

Grantors information goes here

Section 4, Legal Clause, All Right Reserved & Other Legal Notes
All rights will revert to author after 3 years, if limited rights are contracted.
E. Speech, Lecture Tours, and Research Papers & Follow Up:
All publications or Grant-products are commonly published on completion, USA Library of Congress, Trade Journals, Or Author's websites, etc.
Contact for individualized contracts
F. for Time Donation, And Charity Events: 1. 5% of Net contracts paid 2. Time by Appointments Only.3. Write Donations Checks to Fakhraie Trust fund / Bahman Fakhraie
G. Any and All Risks or Harms invokes these legal clauses. The Following legal clauses are base minimum, and will not limit all rights and legal protection, with uniform constitutional rights they are implied and accorded. Contractually all rights are implied and accorded. Please, read all the legal notes before using any materials.

G1. In Cases of misuse of these materials, plagiarisms, use to put at risk of harm, or to harm, (Legal, or Etc.) the firm, CEO, FERDT, president: Mr. Bahman Fakhraie, His family members, it will result in $60 million legal action per each event in United States Courts/ any Jurisdictions determined or set by author or a trust set up by Mr. Bahman Fakhraie. Also, use of creative ideas and intellectual properties for any commerce direct or indirect or by proxy, expansions of outlines, attempts to defraud, over charge, harm with illegal acts, misuse of private and confidential materials, information, and properties, letters, checks, e-mails, faxes, any and all communications, and any electronically stored materials and pictures, or false claims against the above entities will be an agreement with and subject to all elements of this contract, and as a user license, without nullifying further and ensuing legal actions or collections, or as directed by the same or authorities. All other contracts are one time contracts and s. t. this contract. Please, notify firm, Mr. Bahman Fakhraie, of all infractions, transactions, or transfer to individuals or to private or government entities in accord with current laws.

G2a. All Costs due to inquiries, related or required business licenses, legal paper works, and hours, all costs related to corrective or reparation publicity, bonding and insurances costs, stock related activities, all costs related to any harm (financial & legal) will be charges to the sources and inquirers, and none to the firm or Bahman Fakhraie, his family, or any and all of their related assets. All attempts to harm, engagements, cashing checks or accepting cash from the same entities is an agreement with all elements of this contract.

G2b. All copy rights associated with written works and further development of all works remains with the author Bahman Fakhraie or his trusts. All development rights are reserved by the same entities.

G3. Any and all unsolicited commercial phone calls, to Mr. Bahman Fakhraie and, his family will result to a minimum of $ 500 per call charged to the source, due and payable in the same month the call is made, all other elements of this contract also apply, all contracts remain subservient to this contract, all costs of collection and legal actions also are added to the bill payable by source and not Bahman Fakhraie and these entities.

G4.All Consultation and coaching involves risks due to market, business, political, etc. costs and damages related to all such risk are paid by individuals or business entities involved and none is implied or taken by Bahman Fakhraie, his family, or any related assets, under any and all conditions. These entities' court fees are $10,000; et minimum.

G5.Uncomfortable conditions, misapplications of any law to harm, harassment, odd-hour calls, etc will be due cause for termination of services without refund, and are actionable per this contract.

§§§§

E. Speech, Lecture Tours, Research Papers & Follow Up:

1. Per Each Event-$ 350,000 +.
2. with Foreign Travel-$ 3,000,000
3. Book/Cash Advance floor Min; Net Royalties ~40%
4. Scripts: /Starting from.....................$ 300,000
5. Movie Script (120+Pages).................$ 3,000,000
6. Or Cash Advance Plus 2% of All Gross paid annually
7. Consultations Fee/Initial charge non-refunded $ 10,000, & ...10 %
8. Business limited ventures, partnerships, etc. .... ≥ 30%
9. Salary executive level I

F. for Time Donation, And Charity Events: 1. 5% of Net contracts paid 2. Time by Appointments Only.3. Write Donations Checks to Fakhraie Trust fund / Bahman Fakhraie. G. Any and All Risks or Harms invokes these legal clauses. The Following legal clauses are base minimum, and will not limit all rights and legal protection, with uniform constitutional rights they are implied and accorded. Contractually all rights are implied and accorded. Please, read all the legal notes before using any materials. G1. In Cases of misuse of these materials, plagiarisms, use to put at risk of harm, or to harm, (Legal, or Etc.) the firm, CEO: Mr. Bahman Fakhraie, His family members, will result in $60 million legal action per each event in United States Courts/Jurisdictions determine by author or a trust set up by Mr. Bahman Fakhraie. Also, use of creative ideas intellectual properties, expansions of outlines, attempts to defraud, over charge, harm with illegal acts, misuse of private and confidential materials and properties, letters, e-mails, faxes, any and all communications, and any electronically stored materials and pictures, or false claims against the above entities will be an agreement with all elements of this contract, and as a use license, without nullifying ensuing legal actions or collections, or as directed by the same or authorities. Please, notify firm, Mr. Bahman Fakhraie, of all infractions, transactions, or transfer to individuals or to private or government entities. G2a. All Costs due to inquiries, related or required business licenses, legal paper works and hours, all costs related to corrective or reparation publicity, bonding and insurances costs, stock related activities, all costs related to any harm (financial & legal) will be charges to the sources and inquirers, and none to the firm or Bahman Fakhraie, his family, or any and all of their related assets. All attempts to harm, engagements, cashing checks or accepting cash from the same entities is an agreement with all elements of this contract. G2b. All copy rights associated with written works and further development of all works remains with the author Bahman Fakhraie or his trusts. Any and all development rights are reserved by the same entities. G3. Any and all unsolicited commercial phone calls to Mr. Bahman Fakhraie, his family will result to a minimum of $ 500 per call charged to the source, due and payable in the same month the call is made, all other elements of this contract also apply, all contracts remain subservient to this contract, all costs of collection and legal actions also are added to the bill payable by source and not Bahman Fakhraie and these entities. G4.All Consultation and coaching involves risks due to market, business, political, etc. costs and damages related to all such risk are paid by individuals or business entities involved and none is implied or taken by Bahman Fakhraie, his family, or any related assets, under any and all conditions. These entities' court fees are $10,000; et minimum. G5.Uncomfortable conditions, misapplications of any law to harm, harassment, odd-hour calls, etc. will be due cause for termination of services without refund, and are actionable per this contract.

§§§§

Letter of Agreement with FRDET and Fakhraie Bahman

I/We (Ms., Mrs., Mr.): ....

Business Name: ....

Social Security numbers: ....../......./........... ..../......./...............

Tax ID Numbers: ....

Driver License Numbers:

....

Passport (Birth Certificate) Numbers:

....

Have read all the information supplied by Dr. Bahman Fakhraie, and /or FRDET (Trust, LLP). Agree to supply all correct financial and related information and select the following services by marking (X), or Letter a b c, Or Number 1 2 3, or write and specify. Agree to the power of attorney required to confirm or acquire financial and related information. Plus a check for $3000, for preliminary registrations, legal and financial inquiries, and licensing fees.

1: ☐ 2: ☐ 3: ☐ 4: ☐ 5: ☐ 6: ☐ 7: ☐ 8: ☐

Specify which kinds of the following accounts you will require:

Individual/Gov. ☐ Joints ☐ Joint with survival rights ☐ Trusts ☐

Details: ....

Business types:

Ltd Partnership (LLP, LLC) ☐ Soul Owner ☐

Inc/Gov ☐ Firm ☐

Details: ....

I/We agree to pay the fees and costs as they accrue, after 30 days a charge of %10 per annum is added to past due amounts until they are settled or paid in full. That at least 75% charges and expenses are paid no later than six month after initial reports or outlines are examined. That all travel lodgings and phone charges, legal research, and research hours, I/We request are fully paid. I/We have read and understand the nature of business, business cycles, market price fluctuation risks, currency fluctuation risks, social and political risks, natural and climatic risks, and all other risks herewith not itemized; therefore, I/we accept all financial losses, responsibilities, all punitive or compensatory damages that occur for all activities that are undertaken based on or claimed related to the report or reports, advise and etc., generated by Money Wise Firm, Bahman Fakhraie or all the entities named, agents, and associates. I/We understand in cases of any false, misleading, or withholding information the Money Wise Firm and all entities named above will not be held accountable, responsible, financially or otherwise, and will be refunded for any damages fully. I/We release all others associated with Money Wise Firm, and Bahman Fakhraie from financial losses, responsibilities, all compensatory and punitive charges concerning activities I/We undertake.

Sign (full name, titles, and address)

Business (Name, Address; Agents' title):

Section 5, Organization Chart

⇔Requests for grants, grant and contract proposals and Minimums contracted output Grant Funds,

⇓ Organization DUNS, University DUNS ⇓

Administrator ⇒FRDAT

⇓

FERDAT & FERDAT- C

Publishing and Production

President, Administrator, Executive level 1

⇓

Bahman Fakhraie, PhD, © 2011, UOU, UT, USA

®, ™

Tasks and controls, TQC, and Redo, Recycles

⇔Tax and expense disbursements

⇓

Completed project Vs. Minimums contracted output

⇔ Informal notification of source of funds, with future project proposal if any,

⇒Formal and final notification from FRDET, FERDAT

⇔ Final confirmation of conclusion from Administrators

⇒ Final confirmation of conclusion from Organization Fakhraie

⇔ Keeping communication and network open to future project.

Bahman Fakhraie, PhD, © ® ™ 2010-, UOU, UT, USA

Section 6, DATA MANAGEMENT:

Relevant data will be managed, and stored. Moreover, the data and the progression of data used will be stored post completion. As a common practice, Dr. Bahman Fakhraie will, also preserve a historical over view of data for legal purposes, for future use. A portion of that will be shared if requested in written form, post settlement of all expenses. The ethical requirements will be followed in accordance with the applied law established.

The final product will be shared with the grantors, after all the financial settlements have been met. The reviewers will have access to a portion of the progress. All publications or Grant-products are published on completion for academic and educational research, USA Library of Congress, trade journals, FERDAT Publishing, author's websites, other academic journals, etc.

All rights will revert to author after 3 years, if contract exits for limited rights.

Labor laws and benefit distribution will be according to the institutional Fed Cap limits, private contracts; vendors are responsible for their own legal obligations. (Publication Ink, FedExx, kinkcos, vendors etc.)

CPA and Legal establishment, outside to this entity will be contracted to handle more complex issues when they arise, all cost are due, prior to any such required actions are requested.

Full transparencies are practiced for authorized agents only, mostly through the internet, after proper signatures are obtained. All copyrights and proprietary rights are granted, accorded and reserved to Dr. Bahman Fakhraie,

All future development, educational development will have to be contracted, or signed out temporarily, they will revert to Dr. Bahman Fakhraie, in case of all legal issues.

These and other clauses will be amended and upgraded as required over time, they all apply.
Absolut or required non-disclosures by the firm or Dr. Fakhraie will require pre-paid plan with minimum flooring pay. Flex-legalism targeted at the firm, or Dr. B. Fakhraie will be due cause for nonpaid termination by the same.
G. Any and All Risks or Harms invokes these legal clauses. The Following legal clauses are base minimum, and will not limit all rights and legal protection, with uniform constitutional rights they are implied and accorded. Contractually all rights are implied and accorded. Please, read all the legal notes before using any materials.

Sec 7, Check CURRICULUM VITA

SELECTED BIBLIOGRAPHY

Bailey, Martin J. *National Income and the Price Level: A Study in Macroeconomic Theory,* New York, McGraw-Hill, 1971.

Baumol, William J. *Economic Theory and Operational Analysis,* 4th ed., New Jersey: Prentice-Hall, 1977.

Blaug, Mark, *Economic Theory in Retrospect,* 3rd Ed., London: The Cambridge University Press, 1978.

Böhn_Bawerk, Eugen Von. *Capital and Interest: Positive Theory of Capital,* vol. II, Trans. G. D. Hunt & H. F. Sennholz, Chicago: Libertarian Press, 1959.

Boulding, Kenneth E. *Economics As A science*, New York: McGraw-Hill Book Company, 1970.

Byers, Lloyd L. *Concept of Strategic Management: Planning and Implementation*, New York: Harper & Row Publishers

Caves, Richard E. and Jones, R. W. *World Trade and Payments: An Introduction,* 2nd ed. Boston, Little, Brown and Company, 1977

Chiang, Alpha C. *Fundamental Methods of Mathematical Economics*, 2nd ed., New York: McGraw-Hill Book Company, 1974.

Coombs, Philip H. *The World Educational Crisis: A System Analysis*, London: Oxford University Press, 1968.

Domar, Evsey D. *Essays in the Theory of Economic Growth*, New York: Oxford University Press, 1957, 154-167, 168, 181.

Druker, Peter F. *Innovation and Entrepreneurship*, New York: Harper & Row Publishers, 1985.

Eisner, R. "Depreciation Allowances, Replacement Requirement, and Growth," *The American Economic Review*, XLII, December 1952.

Dr. Bahman Fakhraie, *Teconomics of Dynamic Risks All Natural Disasters, And Energy Resource...*
ISBN/EAN13: 0985295856 / 978098529585
https://www.createspace.com/4282704

EBook link: http://www.amazon.com/Teconomics-oF-Dynamic-Risks-ebook/dp/B00CUNPJZ6/ref=sr_1_1?s=digital-text&ie=UTF8&qid=1368893440&sr=1-1&keywords=Dr+bahman+fakhraie

Bahman Fakhraie, PhD., *TECONOMICS,*
ISBN/EAN13: 0985295813 / 9780985295813,
https://www.createspace.com/4196760

—. *TECONOMIC OF VERBALISM,* Utah, FERDAT publishing 2012, and
Paperback link is at, https://www.createspace.com/4121720
The EBook Link is at,
http://www.amazon.com/dp/B00B1LO7UQ
Books web page at, http://bahfecon.wix.com/bahfecon#

—. The Demand and Supply Sides of Appropriate Technological Advancement, (Research paper at University of Utah Economics Dept. 2003)

—. *Demand and supply Sides of Technological Injections*, Utah, FERDAT Publishing, 2004, And at, http://www.amazon.com/dp/098529583X/ref=rdr_ext_tmb #reader_098529583X

—. *Technological injection, dynamic new capital measurements, and Production Theory in Economics*, (Michigan: ProQuest LLC, 2010) and, https://order.proquest.com/OA_HTML/pqdtibeCCtpItmDsp Rte.jsp

—. Books, paperbacks & EBooks web page, http://bahfecon.wix.com/bahfecon#

—. *Teconomics of Verbalism*, Utah FERDAT Publishing 2012, and at, https://www.createspace.com/4121720, Books web page at, http://bahfecon.wix.com/bahfecon#

—. *Analytical Remedies for The Millennial Cascading Economic Declines,* Utah FERDAT Publishing 2012, and at, https://www.createspace.com/4187823,
Books web page at, http://bahfecon.wix.com/bahfecon

—. "Economic Theories and Practices in Technological Changes, capital measures, and Production." (Research paper at University of Utah Economics Dept. 1988)

—. "Hallowing headless nations: the need to invest on public education under the 1980s international economic conditions," (Research paper at University of Utah Economics Dept. 1988)

—. "Transfer of Technologies and Socioeconomic Theories of Dualism," (Research paper at University of Utah Economics Dept. 1983)

Friedman, Milton and Schwartz, Anna Jacobson, *The Great Contraction 1929-1933*, vol.2, 2nd ed., New Jersey: Princeton University Press, 1973

Gander, James Patrick, *Technological Change and Raw Materials*, Salt Lake City: Bureau of Economic and Business Research, University of Utah, 1977.

Gardner, Ackley, *Macroeconomics: Theory and Policy*, New York: Macmillan Publishing Co., 1978.

Girton, Lance and Roper Don, "Theory and Implication of Currency Substitution," *Journal of Money, Credit, and Banking,* 13, no. 1 (February 1981): 12-30.

Hayek, Friedrich August Von. "Kapitalaufzehrung." Weltwirtschaftliches Archive 36, 1932, II, 86-108.

Heilbroner, Robert L. *The Worldly Philosophers*, New York: Time Inc., Special Ed., 1962.

Hicks, Sir John, *The Crisis in Keynesian Economics*, New York: Basic Books, Inc. 1974.

Hirshleifer, Jack, *Investment, Interest, and Capital*, New Jersey: Prentice-Hall, 1970.

—. *Time, Uncertainty, and Information*, New York: Basil Blackwell, 1989.

—. *Price Theory and Applications*, New Jersey: Prentice-Hall, 1976.

Henderson, J. M. and Quandt, R. E. *Microeconomic Theory; A Mathematical Approach*, 2nd ed., New York: McGraw-Hill, 1972. 191-199, 280

Hunt, E. K. and Howard J. Sherman, Economics*: An Introduction to Traditional and Radical Views*, 2nd Ed., San Francisco: Harper and Row Publishers, 1975.

Hutchinson, H. D. *Money, Banking, And The United States Economy*, 3rd. ed. New jersey, Englewood Cliffs, Prentice-Hall, Inc. 1975

Intriligator, Michael D. *Econometric Models, Techniques, and Applications*, New Jersey: Prentice-Hall, 1978.

Johnson, J. *Econometric Methods*. New York: McGraw-Hill, 1972.

Kant, Immanuel, *Critique of Judgment*, Trans. J. H. Bernard, New York: Hafner, 1951.

Kennedy Charles and Thirlwall, A.P. "Surveys in Applied Economics: Technological Progress," *The Economic Journal*, March 1972: 12.

Keynes, John Maynard, *Essays in Biography*, London: The Cambridge University Printing House for Royal Economic Society, 1972.

—. *The General Theory of Employment, Interest and Money,* 1st ed. 1936, London: The Cambridge University Printing House for Royal Economic Society, Reprint 1973.

Kindleberger, Charles P. *The World in Depression 1929-1939*, Los Angeles: University of California Press, 1973.

Kirzner, I.M. *Discovery and the Capitalist Process*, Chicago: University of Chicago Press, 1985.

Klein, P. A. and Moore, G. H., *Monitoring Growth Cycles in Market-Oriented Countries*, (Mass.: published for N. B. E. R., by Ballinger publishing Co., 1985).

Knight, Farnk H. *Risk, Uncertainty and Profit*, Chicago: University of Chicago Press, 1985.

Landes, David S. *The wealth and poverty of nations: Why Some are So Rich and Some are So Poor*, (New York: W.W. Norton & Company, 1998).

Lindert, Peter H. and Kindleberger Charles P., *International Economics,* 7th Ed., Illinois: Richard Irwin, 1982.

Mansfield, Edwin, *Technological Change*, New York: W. W. Norton & Co., 1971.

Mark, Blaug, *Economic Theory in Retrospect*, 3rd Ed. London: The Cambridge University Press, 1978.

Marx, K. (In a letter he wrote to Engel, dated 20 August, 1862, London), (handout by Professor Randa, 2004)

McKinnon, Ronald I. *Money and Capital in Economic Development*, Washington D. C.: The Brookings Institution, 1973.

Mensch, Gerhard, Das *technilogische Patt.*, Frankfurt: Umschau Verlag, 1975.

—, *Stalemate in Technology: innovation overcome the Depression*, (Massachusetts: Ballinger Publishing Company, 1979).

Miles, T.R. "Gestalt Theory," in The Encyclopedia of Philosophy, New York: Macmillan Publishing Co., vols. 3 and 4, 1967.

Mishan, Edward Joshua, *Cost-Benefit Analysis,* 4th Ed. London: Unwin Hyman, 1988.

Moran, Michael. "New England Transcendentalism," in The Encyclopedia of Philosophy, (New York: Macmillan Publishing Co., Vols. 3 and 4, 1967).

Mundell, Robert A. "Growth, Stability, and Inflationary Finance," Journal *of Political Economy*, 73, 1963.

Pindyck, R.S. and Rubinfeld, D.L., *Econometric Models and Econometric*, 2nd ed., New York: McGraw-Hills, 1981.

Ott, J. Steven, *The Organizational Culture Perspectives*, (Pacific Grove, California: Brooks/Cole Publishing Company, 1989).

Quirk, James and Saposnik, Rubin, *Introduction to General Equilibrium Theory and Welfare Economics*, New York: McGraw-Hill, 1968.

Rima, Ingrid, *Development of Economic Analysis*, 7th ed., New York: Routledge, 2009.

Rodinson, M. *Islam and Capitalism*, Trans. B. Pearce, Austin: University of Texas, 1981.

Rosenberg, Nathan, Technology *and American Economic Growth*, New York: M. E. Sharp, 1972.

Ruttan, V. W. "Usher and Schumpeter on Invention, and Technological Change," Quarterly *Journal of Economics*, 1960, 602

Ruttan, Vernon W. "Usher and Schumpeter on Invention, Innovation, and Technological change," Quarterly *Journal of Economics*, 1960, 73

Samuelson, Anthony Paul. *Economics*, 11th Ed., New York: McGraw-Hill, 1980.

Savich, R.S. and Thomson, L. A. *Resource Allocation within the Product Life Cycles*, Business Topic, MSU: MSU, fall 1978.

Schmooker, Jacob, *Invention and Economic Growth*, Massachusetts: Harvard University Press, 1966.

Schultz, Theodore W. *Investing in People: The Economics of Population Quality*, Berkley: University of California Press, 1982.

Schumpeter, Joseph A. *Business Cycles*, vol. 1. New York: McGraw Hill Book Company, 1939.

—. *Business Cycles: A Theoretical, Historical, and Statistical Analysis of the Capitalists Process,* vol. I, New York, McGraw Hill Book Company, 1938.

—. *The Theory of Economic Development: An Inquiry into Profits, Capital, Credit, Interest, and Business Cycle*, Trans., Redvers Opie, London: Oxford University Press, Reprint 1980.

Smith, Adam. *An Inquiry into the Nature and Cause of Wealth of Nations*, Edited by E. Cannon, Chicago: University of Chicago Press, 1976.

—. *An Inquiry into the Nature and Causes of Wealth of Nations*, vol. 2, 2nd ed., Oxford: the Clarendon Press, 1988.

—. *The Theory of Moral Sentiments*, London, 1st ed., 1757.

Smith, E.J. Chambers, R.H. Scott and R.S. *National Income Analysis and Forecasting*, Glenview: Scott, Foresman and Company, 1975.

Spiegle, Henry William. *The Growth of Economic thought*, North Carolina: Duke University Press, 1983.

Stigler, George J. *The Theory of Price*, 3rd ed., New York: The Macmillan Company, 1966.

Takaki, Ronald, *A Different Mirror: A History of Multicultural America*, London: Little Brown and Company, 1993.

Taylor, John R., *An Introduction to Error Analysis*, Mill Valley: University Science Books, 1982.

Thirtle, Colin G. and Ruttan V. W. *The Role of Demand and Supply in the Generation of Diffusion of Technological Change*, Switzerland, 1987.

U. S. President, *Economic Report of the President*, (Washington, D.C.: Government printing office, 1990)

Usher, Abbot Payson, *A History of Mechanical Inventions*, London: Oxford University Press, 1954.

Usher, Abbot Payson, *A History of Mechanical Inventions,* Revised ed., London: Oxford University Press, 1954.

Viner, Jacob, *Studies in the Theories of International Trade*, New York: Harper and Brothers publishers, 1937.

Wainwright, A. C. Chiang and K., *Fundamental Methods of Mathematical Economics*, 4th ed., Boston: McGraw-Hill Irwin, 2005.

Webster, Merriam, *Merriam-Webster's Collegiate Dictionary*, 9th ed., Springfield: M.W. Inc., 1985.

Young, Hugh D. *Statistical Treatment of Experimental Data*, New York: McGraw-Hill, 1962.

CURRICULUM VITA

Bahman Fakhraie, PhD, UOU, UT, USA
University Of Utah, Economic Dept., U. O. U.; Salt Lake City, Utah USA, 84112
Permanent Address: c/o 1120 Canyon Rd No. 29; Ogden Utah 84404
E-Mail: bf9@utah.edu , bahf.econ@gmail.com, dr.bahf.econ@gmail.com
Dr. Bahman Fakhraie's Books webpage, http://bahfecon.wix.com/bahfecon
Honors and Awards: **Omicron Delta Epsilon Honor Society**
Utah State U. USA, **Certificates Keys to Agricultural Development at the Local Level**
Student Leadership Positions: **President of International Student Association** [ASUSU]
Bachelor of Science: **Utah State University**
Master of Science: **Utah State University**
PhD, University of Utah **University of Utah**
PhD, Economics (international economics), University of Utah
Certificate of Completion, PhD in Economics University of Utah, 2010
Certificate of Completion, PhD in Economics University of Chicago, 2011

Mission Statement:

To formulate optimum functionality in management teams, in order to make profitable and beneficial contributions, and create opportunity for merited advancements.
Utilizing rare combination of theory and empiricism, cultivated in multi-cultural inclusive settings in academic and private enterprise, I enhance the productivity and completion of project management. Experiences, among fields of International Trade, Managerial, and Production

theories in Economics, Finance, and Business, which modern business and academic institutions find very expensive to employ and too costly not to employ. The extensive background helps advance research in my field of study.

Goals:

I have initiated, passed, and funded many constructive projects --goals by committees--, where it has been value enhancing and mutually beneficial individually, and by team assists. Private Senior Economist: Research Positions with Contracts, Teaching, Research, Books, with contract.

Short Term Private Contracts are for economic and financial educational consultations.

Academic Preparatory Continuum:

PhD, University of Utah, Dissertation:

TECHNOLOGICAL INJECTION, DYNAMIC NEW CAPITAL MEASUREMENTS AND PRODUCTION THEORY IN ECONOMICS

Thesis statement:

The dynamic influences of technology and elemental factors of production --defined and measured in this dissertation-- are greater than commonly have been calculated or expected. The impacts of different measurements of capital stocks (traditional and new adjusted capital) on embodied and disembodied technological variables, on productivity, and economic growth of national social products are tested. The econometric effects of two new capital stock measures introduced in the writing of Friedrich August Von Hayek, John Maynard Keynes, and further developed by Evsey D. Domar, and ignored by most modern economists are examined. Therefore, we focus on the demand and supply side of technological embodied in capital, in human skill and produced goods and services, and the economy. Dr. Bahman Fakhraie's Book-link is at, https://order.proquest.com/OA_HTML/pqdtibeCCtpItmDspRte.jsp

Post-Doctoral Research and Goals:

1. Updating the econometrics of the dissertation to most recent available data and dates, (per available grants)
2. Include, countries, with acceptable data in the study, set up formulaic development in excel etc. for use. (per grants)
3. Focus on the theoretical advancement in production processes for systemic innovational additive methodologies, in Movie production, Agriculture, and other creative industries, using existing or newly hired faculties, in anchored and linked institutions. This is a great serious work in shadows of Adam Smith, Schumpeter, Hayak, and Keynes.

Teconomics: Scientific Synthesis of Economics and Technology in Teconomics

4. Stream line methodologies, and project for PhD Students, master students, and introductory fields' level, an extension of the dissertation and current copyrighted writings.
5. A multimedia production of Dr. Fakhraie's recent research,
   NEW DYNAMIC ECONOMIC MODELS TO STUDY TECHNOLOGY INJECTIONS & DYNAMIC CAPITAL FORMATION, IMPACTS ON INTERNATIONAL TRADE, EXCHANGE RATE, AND GLOBAL ECONOMIC OPTIMASATION

   Presentation by Dr. Bahman Fakhraie
6. Of course, this will be under Sec G of private contract and without infringing on rights of marketing, publishing, and distribution of the same.

Certain contracts will be more
restrictive, including specific names.

7. Finish the books series in post dissertation Teconomic studies, Micro, Macro, Teconometrics, Teconomic Analysis, and Political Teconomics. (in progress)

Books, published: DR. Bahman Fakhraie's Books web page at, http://bahfecon.wix.com/bahfecon

Dr. Bahman Fakhraie, *TECONOMIC OF VERBALISM,* Utah, FERDAT publishing 2012, a
Paperback link is at, https://www.createspace.com/4121720
The EBook Link is at,
http://www.amazon.com/dp/B00B1LO7UQ
Books web page at, http://bahfecon.wix.com/bahfecon

- *Demand and supply Sides of Technological Injections*, Utah, FERDAT Publishing, 2004, And at, http://www.amazon.com/dp/098529583X/ref=rdr_ext_tmb reader_098529583X

- *Teconomics: the microeconomic analysis*, Utah, FERDAT publishing 2012, and, https://www.createspace.com/4196760, Books web page at, http://bahfecon.wix.com/bahfecon

- *Technological injection, dynamic new capital measurements, and Production Theory in Economics*, (Michigan: ProQuest LLC, 2010) and, https://order.proquest.com/OA_HTML/pqdtibeCCtpItmDspRte.jsp

Books web page at,
http://bahfecon.wix.com/bahfecon

- *Teconomics of Verbalism*, Utah FERDAT Publishing 2012, and at, https://www.createspace.com/4121720, Books web page at, http://bahfecon.wix.com/bahfecon

- *Analytical Remedies for The Millennial Cascading Economic Declines,* Utah FERDAT Publishing 2012, and at, https://www.createspace.com/4187823,

- "The Demand and Supply Sides of Appropriate Technological Advancement." (Research paper at University of Utah Economics Dept. 2003),

- "Economic Theories and Practices in Technological Changes, capital measures, and Production." (Research paper at University of Utah Economics Dept. 1988).
- Fakhraie, Bahman, "The Demand and Supply Sides of Appropriate Technological Advancement." (Research paper at University of Utah Economics Dept. 2003).
- "Hallowing headless nations? The need to invest on public education under the 1980s international economic conditions," (Research paper at University of Utah Economics Dept. 1988).
- "Transfer of Technologies and Socioeconomic Theories of Dualism," (Research paper at University of Utah Economics Dept. 1983).

Production theory in Agriculture

Agro-production, Sheep production in Iran (an onsite research project 1975)
Monetary Macroeconomic Specialization (Milton Freedman,)
International Monetary macroeconomic Specializations (Robert Mundell)
Fiscal Analysis of oscillatory modifications
Applied Agricultural production in developing economies
Inappropriate Technology Transfers by Corporations and dualistic induced instabilities in a pre-democratic economies.
Certificate in Rural Development from Utah State University
Research Skills:
Statistical packages, data selection, analysis, and formulations.
Computer Languages, Spread Sheet Data Analysis, Writings
Multimedia & Creative Skills: Film and video production, CD: audio and video works
Languages: Fluent in English and Farsi, I can read and write some French, and Arabic.
Fluent in Dezfili Dari dialectic [One of the earliest spoken languages]
Teaching Experiences:
University of Utah: macroeconomic and microeconomic: introductory course, and related mathematics.
Utah State University: Economic Department, Persian language, and cultural studies to faculty and students, and teaching assistance for Agricultural economics.
Volunteer Helping of other students
Student leadership positions AUSU, as an undergraduate
PROFESSIONAL EXPERIENCE:
Founder and Management of Money Wise Firm (A Private Financial Education Foundation for Personal Financial studies), 1970 to date

Volunteer work: President; V.P., and Treasurer of Cherrywood Association Inc., multimillion dollars project, (Different 3 year cycles 1980 to 1999, consultation to date)
Real Estate Investor and Renovations, General Manger, to date
Agribusiness management, owner manager
Auto Agency sale manager/sold
Auto shop management/sold
Numerous Volunteer Projects: planning, budgeting, contracting, and finishing.
Beside educational publications, and digital multi-media CDS, DVD formats, copyrighted at USA the library of congress.

Other Experience:

Budget Analysis, Budget Setting, Budget Forecasting, Asset Allocation Studies, Portfolio Analysis Studies, Saving (Goal Setting) Plan, Tax Management Studies, Risk/Reward Management and studies, Economic Condition risk Analysis, Managerial Goal Setting and Project Production Process and Enactments.

Economic Topics of Research and Lectures:
Non-Marxist Revolutions in Middle East (Iran)
Economic and Indices (Measurement Issues)
Economic Theories of Technological Changes and Capital Measures
Technological Change, Growth Rate, and Capital Formations with US Data
Education and Taxation
Hollowing Headless Nations! Education Crisis
Technological Parameters Statistical Measurements
New Econometric Measurements of Capital in Production Theory

Reading (Economic, Science, Mathematics, Econometrics, Statistics, Mystery, Ancients), Films (art, industry), Jazz, Foreign Eclectics music, Fly-fishing

BOOK PROMOTIONS

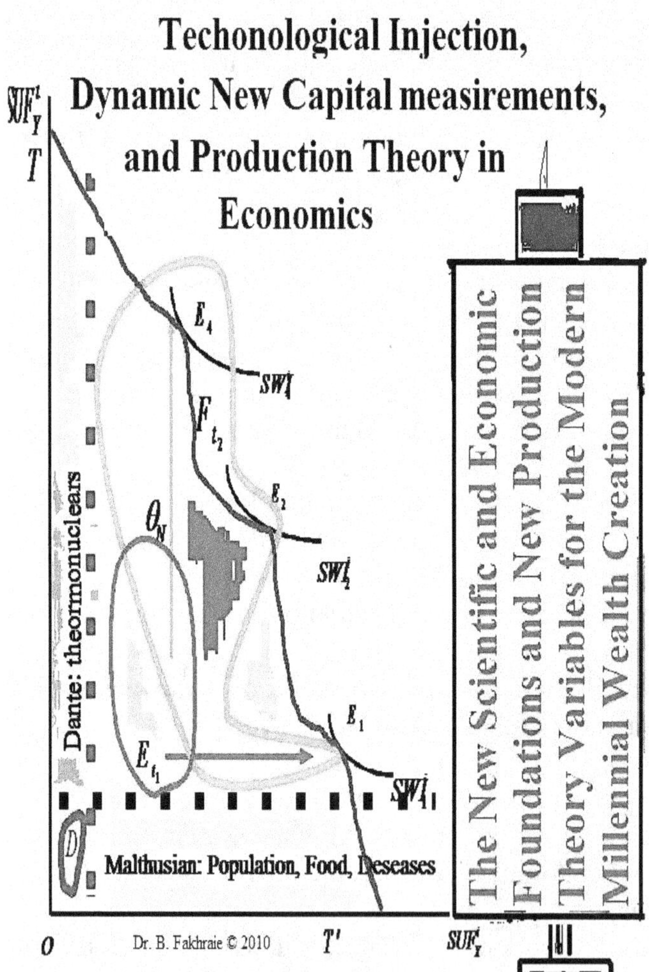

DEMAND & SUPPLY SIDES OF TECHNOLOGICAL INJECTIONS

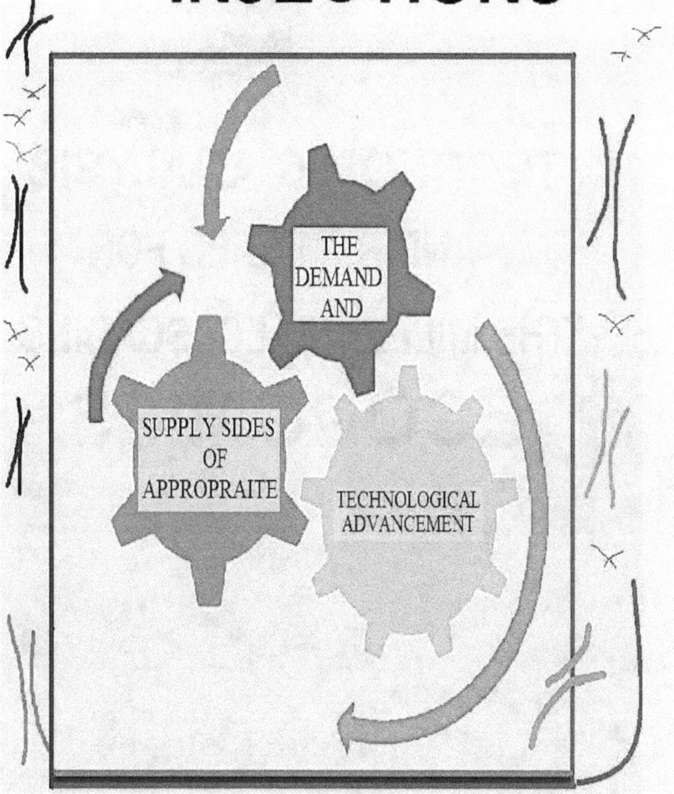

Dr. Bahman Fakhraie's books web page link,
http://bahfecon.wix.com/bahfecon

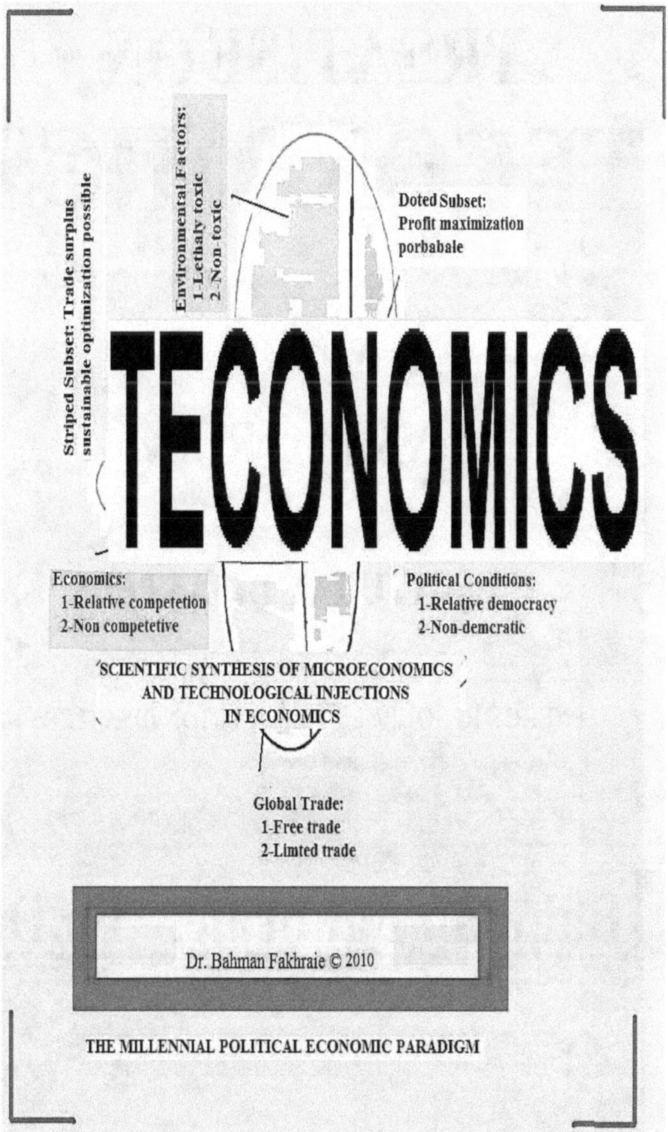

Book link, https://www.createspace.com/4196760

TREATISE ON
TECONOMICS
ØF
DYNAMIC RISKS

ALL NATURAL DISASTERS,

&

ENERGY RESOURCES PRODCUTION DISASTERS

Bahman Fakhraie, Ph.D.

https://www.createspace.com/4187823

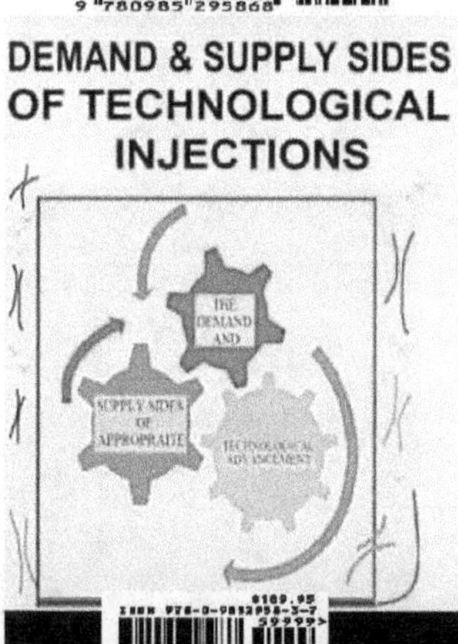

Please contact FERDAT PUBLISHING C/O dr.bahf.econ@gmail.com with your DISCOVER, VISA, OR MASTER CARD. All sales are final (no refunds), postages, FEDEX, UPS, grounds with trace will be added. (All costs or legal costs will also be added). There is a temporary promotional, first four books for $999. Sorry, all unrelated communications will be spammed, without replay.

Dr. Bahman Fakhraie's books,

http://bahfecon.wix.com/bahfecon